THE BIRTH OF THE CONSTITUTION

An Informal History

NOVELS

The Wickedest Pilgrim
Reluctant Cavalier
His Majesty's Highwayman
This Bright Sword
Captain Bashful
Lord of the Isles
Captain Adam
Stronghold
Panama Passage
Nobody Heard the Shot
Each One Was Alone
Weeping is for Women
Pistols in the Morning

BIOGRAPHY

Elizabeth I
John the Great:
The Times and Life of John L. Sullivan
The Gentleman from New York:
A Biography of Roscoe Conkling
Sir Humphrey Gilbert
Bonnie Prince Charlie
Sir Walter Raleigh
Marlborough

HISTORY

The Battle of New Orleans:
An Informal History of the War That Nobody Wanted: 1812
Valley Forge
July 4, 1776
Victory at Yorktown
Goodbye to Gunpowder

JUVENILE

Rod Rides High

THE BIRTH
OF THE CONSTITUTION

An Informal History

by
Donald Barr Chidsey

CROWN PUBLISHERS, INC. • NEW YORK

To David Ash Chidsey

10848

Second Printing, August, 1964

CONTENTS

Chapter 1

The Desperate Men

HENRY KNOX did not like what he saw, still less what he sensed in the air. He felt as though he was sitting on the lip of a volcano.

It was not that he was by nature apprehensive, a worrier; for the contrary was true. Henry Knox was fat and positive, a red-faced soldier with damn-you eyes and the very voice of Stentor, a critter who got things done, by God. He had been a bookseller in Boston before the Revolution, and this was hard to believe, for he was so emphatically the person of action, the rough and rugged type, downright, straightforward, thorough. When the shooting had started in '75 he found his proper place—among the guns. The last time he had visited here, western Massachusetts, was in the course of the siege of Boston, when against incredible difficulties and in the depth of winter he had brought the cannons all the way from Fort Ticonderoga to Dorchester peninsula, making it possible for General Washington to chase away General Howe and all his redcoats. Thereafter he had been Washington's chief of artillery, a loud and efficient one, and now that the war was over he was the infant republic's first Secretary of War. He held the rank of major general in the United States Army.

The United States Army consisted of 700 rank and file, plus a few officers; and there were many who insisted, even screamed, that even this was too many, and that the sundry state militias would be ample to keep the peace.

It was in his capacity of Secretary of War that General Knox was in Springfield on September 29, 1786, and most decidedly he did not like what he saw. He feared for the future of the arsenal.

The arsenal had been established in 1777, early in the war, when the Second Continental Congress leased ten acres from the town of Springfield for ninety-nine years. It was on a hill conveniently near the Connecticut River yet far enough from the sea to insure it against raiding parties sent ashore from warships of the all-powerful British Navy. Once it had consisted of wooden buildings—storehouses, barracks, repair shops, a foundry for the casting of brass field pieces—but recently a strong brick magazine had been built, a little fort in itself, solid, firm. The whole place, as General Knox well knew, contained 450 tons of military stores, including 1,300 barrels of gunpowder, 7,000 muskets, and much shot and shell.

Those muskets were brand new, and each was equipped with a brand-new bayonet. The men who roamed the streets of Springfield, twirling their bludgeons, or who stood in sullen groups before the courthouse, where they leaned on dung forks or on ancient fowling pieces, would have loved to get their hands on the muskets of the arsenal.

There had been demonstrations, some orderly, others less orderly. The mutterers asked for the suppression of the State Senate, an unsympathetic set of appointed, not elected, mossbacks. They asked that the lower courts be constrained from sitting, lest the already overcrowded jails be crammed yet more with debtors—in other words, they asked for a moratorium. They asked that lawyers' fees and fees for law enforcement be lowered. ("Your fees for criminal executions are too high, for one thing," a member of a street crowd shouted to Sheriff Greenleaf in Worcester, just after Greenleaf had read the riot act. "If you think my fees are too high you need not wait long for redress," the sheriff snapped, "for I'll hang every one of you with the greatest of pleasure—and without charge.") They asked for a fairer share of the governmental machinery in the northern and western counties, for they complained that Boston held all of the power. Most vociferously of all, and ignoring the disastrous experiences of so many other states, they demanded an issue of paper money, so that there would be enough to go around. They were desperate men.

General Knox was not interested in their woes, for his was an aristocratical turn of mind, but he was very much interested in their intentions, and with his nose for trouble he smelled the nearness of out-and-out war. It had been explained to him that the dissidents, almost all of them small farmers, fell into two general classes, mobbers and conventioneers. The conventioneers had called or were calling a series of irregularly formed meetings, at some of which as many as fifty towns were represented. These were unofficial, informal, and in deadly earnest. They made no threats, and the delegates carried no weapons. Customarily each convention would start by proclaiming itself to be "a lawful and constitutional body," and by disavowing any thought of violence. It would then draw up a list of grievances—as many as seventeen in one case, at Worcester in August—and forward these, in the form of a petition, to the state legislature, where they did no good.

The mobbers were direct-action men, young and truculent, at first the riffraff of the western and northern counties, who more than once had threatened and on a few occasions actually had succeeded in browbeating a lower court out of sitting. The other day they had gone even further and prevented the sitting, in Worcester, of the Supreme Judiciary Court, for they feared, as it was reported, that they would be indicted by that court on charges of treason.

The trouble was that instead of the conventioneers gradually taking over the mobbers, as had been hoped, the mobbers appeared to be taking over the conventioneers. As the futility of petitioning became plain there were fewer conventions and more mobs. Nor were the mobbers, now, all or even largely loafers. They were organizing. Over on the other side of the river, in West Springfield, a young fellow by the name of Luke Day, who had a brevet majority in the Continental Army, was drilling musket- and broomstick-carrying squads out in the open on the village green every day, afterward sulfurously haranguing them. In and around Pelham another veteran, Daniel Shays, was every bit as open and every bit as belligerent with his own large and obstreperous following. And there were others—Eli Parsons, Job Shattuck, Jacob Parmenter, John Hamlin, most of them, like Shays and Day, veterans of the Revolution. They would be joined by many, many more if ever they lived up to their tavern-table-pounding threats to break open the jails and free the incarcerated debtors.

An explosion, indubitably, was overdue.

Governor Bowdoin[1] was not a man to be intimidated. He called up the militia in Berkshire, Hampden, Hampshire, and Worcester counties; he summoned a special session of the legislature to meet this emergency, and when the emergency became even more acute he moved the date for that special session ahead from October 18 to September 27.

The legislature hardly helped. The rebels—they could be so designated by this time—had not a single friend in the Senate, which refused even to receive their petitions. The House was not nearly so crusty, but it might have been touched by panic, for after a prodigious exhibition of procrastination it allowed itself to accede to a suspension of the writ of habeas corpus, and it went along with the Senate in passing an act that made anybody who attended a "riotous" or "tumultuous" assembly, whether he was armed or unarmed, liable to forfeit all his "lands, tenements, goods and chattels" and also to "be whipped thirty-nine stripes on the naked back, at the public whipping-post, and suffer imprisonment for a term not exceeding twelve months nor less than six months; and once every three months during the said imprisonment receive the same number of stripes on the naked back, at the public whipping-post."

In Springfield, Henry Knox sat down and wrote a warning letter to Governor Bowdoin, holding him responsible for the safety of the arsenal. The governor tossed the responsibility right back at him, insisting that it was up to the federal government to protect its own property. The governor added, however, that he had called out much of the militia, and would call up more.

Should General Knox plead with Congress for troops? Would the men consent to serve, with their pay so sadly in arrears? What would Massachusetts think of an invasion of federal soldiery? For that matter, what would the other leery states think of it? Knox was a troubled man when he went back to New York, the capital of the country just then.

Congress was amenable, though many of its members, like Knox himself, wondered aloud what effect a federal force would have on Massachusetts and the other states. They were saved by an unexpected development.

The Northwest Territory (comprising the present states of Ohio, Illinois, Indiana, Michigan, and Wisconsin) from the beginning had been a problem for the new nation. How should it be opened, in fairness to all, and made to pay for itself, or even to bring some income into the national treasury, which could use it? Many states claimed that territory, as well as the vast territory south of the Ohio River and east of the Mississippi, excepting for the narrow, far-south strip that was in dispute, being claimed by Spain. Thomas Jefferson, the omnipercipient, had given much thought to the matter of these vast western lands, and he had proposed to subdivide them into ten new states, in each of which slavery would be prohibited, for it was Jefferson's belief that if it was contained, and not allowed to spread, slavery would die of its own accord. The southern states refused at first to give up their western holdings, except that Virginia forwent her claims to land north of the Ohio, in which virtually everybody had stakes; and nothing came of Jefferson's plan to create ten new commonwealths, which he would have named Metropotamia, Illinoia, Sylvania, Michigania, Saratoga, Cersonesus, Assenisipia, Washington, Polypotamia, and Pelisipia, for he was a classical scholar.

The government lately had been concentrating on the territory north of the Ohio, which it had proposed to parcel out to war veterans. Surveyors had gone forth, and the Indians, understandably, didn't like that. The surveyors themselves, men who at that time could not possibly have heard of the disturbances in western Massachusetts, gave Congress a needed excuse for raising forces when they reported that the Shawnees, the Potawatomies, the Chippewas, the Tawas, and the Twightwees either were on the warpath or were about to take to that thoroughfare, while many other tribesmen were restless. The surveyors asked for protection.

Congress, then, voted to authorize the raising of 2,040 rank and file,[2] the word to be put forth that these were for the western country, where they would overawe the redskins. How would such a force be paid, Congress being, as Congress always was, penniless? This too was provided for. Congress requisitioned $530,000 in specie, not their own money, from all of the states, and optimistically it proposed to raise a 6 per cent interest loan of $500,000 on this, if it ever got any of it. There was nothing in the Articles of Confederacy to enable Congress to collect from the states, which habitually ignored such requests. In this case the only state that made any move to pay was Virginia, where they were worried about those Indians.

It might have struck some as a suspicious circumstance that the Congress stipulated that except for two small groups of cavalrymen to be raised in Virginia and Maryland, horsy states, all of the hoped-for recruits were to come from New England. Perhaps nobody cared. It was not the custom to take Congress very seriously.

After having passed this momentous legislation, that body ceased to function at all for a while, since it could not get together enough members to make up a quorum. This often happened. When Major General William Shepard of the Massachusetts militia, who had between 800 and 900 poorly armed men at Springfield, wrote to the Secretary of War for permission to use some of the arsenal weapons, General Knox was obliged to answer that he couldn't give such permission without the agreement of Congress, which body was in a state of suspension. General Shepard risked his career and took the weapons anyway.

The attack on the arsenal did not come just then. But the war was under way all the same.

Job Shattuck had been the first casualty. He had led a notably disreputable mob at Concord, camping on the green for several days, many of his men drunk, but he ran away when some east Massachusetts units of militia started toward him from Cambridge, and he was trapped in a wood near Groton, his home town, and wounded several times when he put up a fight.

Shays was in general command of the insurgent forces, though he was junior to Luke Day in years, rank, and military experience, besides being no hand at oratory—an important accomplishment, Day's specialty. He was at Worcester with a force estimated at more than 1,000, and talking of a descent upon Cambridge, perhaps even on wicked Boston itself. The trouble was, he couldn't feed his men, and he was loath to make an impost on the city. Another trouble was that a large force, which *was* well fed, was approaching him from the east. He retreated to Rutland. That was December 9; and the weather was such that the militia did not pursue.

On January 19 an even larger force of militia began to assemble, at Roxbury, under General Benjamin Lincoln. No more than the federal Congress did the Commonwealth of Massachusetts have cash to spare, nor was the Legislature any longer in session; and without money the men would not march. Lincoln raised it, some $50,000, almost single-handedly, from wealthy businessmen of Boston and the vicinity. His method was simple. He told them that they had a choice between lending at interest *something* of what they now had (and they were in a position to see that they got it back from the state when things were quiet) and giving it *all* later. The loan was oversubscribed.

Shays fell back toward Springfield, where Shepard was waiting with some 1,100 men, Shays had under his immediate command about that same number, strewn along the Boston Post Road east of the town. Day, across the river, had about 400 men, and Eli Parsons had another 400, all from Berkshire County,

SHAYS' REBELLION

encamped north of Springfield, which thus, except on the south, was surrounded.

Some of the men, on both sides, wore their old Continental Army uniforms, but most were in ordinary everyday attire, superimposed, in the case of militia officers and noncoms, with insignia of rank. Since there was a great deal of shifting back and forth, and many messages were sent, it became imperative to tell foe from friend. This was done, by unspoken agreement, in the classic method of the warrior—by means of hat decoration. The rebels wore a sprig of hemlock, the loyalists a strip of white paper. Cautious travelers, never knowing what group they might fall in with next, carried both.

Shays planned to attack the arsenal straight on, though he must have known that Shepard had field pieces that could mow his men down before they got within musket range. He sent to Day in West Springfield, asking him to join him in the attack, which Day could easily have done, the river being frozen solid. Day replied that he was not able to make it then, January 25, but would be on hand the following day. Shays never got that message; it was intercepted and sent to General Shepard.

Shays' men started toward the arsenal.

Shepard did everything he could to avoid bloodshed. There had been plenty of notes back and forth, and this continued to a point only a few hundred yards from the arsenal. Even when the rebels were within cannon range General Shepard ordered only a volley fired high, over their heads. They wavered, but they came on in. General Shepard ordered a straight-ahead volley.

When the smoke cleared the rebels were seen to be in full, indeed scandalous, flight. They had left on the ground three dead men, Ezekiel Root and Ariel Webster of Gill and Jabez Spicer of Leyden, and one who was dying, John Hunter of Shelburne. The bodies were put into an open stable on the arsenal grounds, where they soon froze stiff, so that when relatives came for them several days later they were in fine condition.

Shays could not get his men to try again, and he proceeded to Chicopee, where he was joined by Parsons and the Berkshire contingent.

On January 27 Lincoln arrived. He crossed the river on the ice, scattered a few pickets, and caused Day to retire hastily to Northampton. Then Lincoln sent a force up the river, "Shad Alley," to keep Day from joining Shays, and at two o'clock the next morning he started after Shays, who by this time had fallen back to South Hadley and Amherst. Shays was less scrupulous now, and he had pretty well cleaned Amherst out of provisions, taking them away in ten sleighs. Lincoln sent a side force to Middlefield, fifty Brookfield men under Colonel Baldwin in sleighs, together with a hundred horsemen under Colonel Crafts. After some dickering they took fifty-nine prisoners and nine laden sleighs. The snow was thick.

It was at Middlefield that one Lieutenant Luddington of the rebels, in charge of a surrounded company in a house, heard his former colonel, now a general, Tupper, call out a demand that he surrender. Luddington had served as a corporal under Tupper all through the Revolution. Habit was strong, and he surrendered. It was that kind of war.

It was not yet over. Despite all sorts of protesting messages back and forth, and many clear professions of a reluctance to draw blood, Shays had to be watched, he had to be disarmed.

He was stationed in two camps on two hills near Pelham, and word came to General Lincoln at noon of the twenty-ninth that these camps appeared to be breaking up. It could be that Shays was only seeking a spot less exposed to the wind and snow, or it could be that he was slipping away. Lincoln put his camp on the alert. At six o'clock came definite information that Shays and all his force had indeed taken the road to Petersham. Within two hours Lincoln was after him.

How the men ever managed those thirty miles—and from New Salem on, the wind was from the north, right in their faces, and snow began to fly again—will never be known. It is likely that they were *afraid* to fall out, knowing that they would freeze.

The surprise at Petersham, just before dawn, was complete.

No shots were fired, and the bulk of the force was taken prisoner, though Shays himself with a handful of followers escaped up a back road toward Athol, eventually to cross the New Hampshire line to Windsor.

Thereafter the rebellion degenerated. There was a notable skirmish at Sheffield, where the rebels lost two dead and thirty hurt, and the militia two dead and one wounded, but for the next month or so there were only scattered raids on small towns and farmhouses. There was some hoodlumism and a great deal of theft committed in the name of military necessity, but there was nothing that could be classed as an atrocity.

Hundreds of men were rounded up and made to swear an oath of allegiance to the Commonwealth of Massachusetts and were deprived of their right to serve on juries or to hold any public office, or yet to sell liquor retail, for three years. Others were tried and sentenced to pay fines, to serve prison terms, to be whipped. Except that one man did stand for one hour on the public gallows with a rope around his neck, not one of these penalties was carried out, and all the rebels in time were pardoned.

None of the top leaders were caught, but fourteen of the minor ones were tried, found guilty, and sentenced to be hanged. These too, in time, were pardoned.

The new federal force never was fully raised, and what there was was soon dissolved, for thanks in part to the activities of George Rogers Clark and in part to the fact that the Indians with characteristic Indianness, couldn't get along together, couldn't agree on any plan of war, *that* danger was past.

Not until February 24, when all the fighting had ceased, did a band of 120 federal soldiers relieve the Massachusetts militiamen as guards at the Springfield arsenal.

But the country had suffered a very bad scare, and it was avowed on all sides by men of sense and sensibility that *something* had to be done.

Something was.

Chapter 2

A Titan Teeters

IT HAD BEEN a long time coming. The Articles of Confederation, fumblingly and hesitantly embraced in war years, set up nothing better than a loose alliance designed to hold the states more or less together in time of crisis: they were not, and never had been, thought of as a centralized, planned system of government. They provided no courts, no executive. They did stipulate a Congress, but they gave to that body little other than advisory powers.

The early Congresses were noble. The sessions of the Stamp Act Congress, the First Continental Congress, and the first years of the Second Continental Congress were attended by some nincompoops but also by many fine, intelligent, dedicated men. Without any justification in law, lacking all precedent, and with their own necks in a noose, these men raised and equipped an army, encouraged states, drew up rules for their own perpetuation, waged a long and trying war, made an alliance with France, and adopted the Declaration of Independence.

That Declaration came early in the life of the Second Continental Congress, which remained in being for many years and which was still functioning at the time of Shays' Rebellion, though it had long since lost the respect of the people.

It was still, on paper, the Second Continental Congress indeed, but it was by no means the group it once had been. The procedures called for were almost incalculably clumsy, and men of spirit grew disgusted with the exercise of such a shadowy jurisdiction, especially in peacetime. Most of the really devoted

18

patriots, the able ones, had switched to serve rather their individual states, where power was real, or had dropped out of
politics altogether. There remained place-seekers, hangers-on.

"What a lot of rascals we had in that Congress," Gouverneur Morris was to write to John Jay, who replied: "We had."

Morris remained in the only organ of government, though
no longer with the old fervor. Jay had become the nation's first
secretary of foreign affairs. Washington was out of public life,
and determined to stay out, the busy, fretful laird of Mount
Vernon. John Adams was ambassador in London, Thomas Jefferson ambassador in Paris. Benjamin Franklin, in his eighties,
was president of the Supreme Executive Council of Pennsylvania. in effect, he was the governor of that state, which, like
Georgia, had a unicameral legislature. Samuel Adams, distrust-
ful of centralized authority, seldom stirred from Boston.
Richard Henry Lee was more interested in the affairs of his
native Virginia than in those of a vacillating, pusillanimous,
wholly contemptible Congress.

Congress had no treasury, as it had no longer any dignity.
It did not even own a home of its own, but went scuttling about
like a squirrel, as it had done during the war. It was a measure
of Congress's weakness when in June of 1783 some eighty-odd
federal soldiers, under their sergeants but without any commis-
sioned officers, marched from their camp at Lancaster, Pennsylvania, to Philadelphia, where Congress at that time was sitting.
The men wanted their pay, and they shouted as much, from
time to time pausing for a swig. It was scarcely an edifying
spectacle. The soldiers would point their muskets at the win-
dows of the old State House, the very building in which the
Declaration of Independence had been decided upon and
signed, and they would threaten to shoot. They did no material
harm, actually, nor did they get their back pay; but they did
scare the Congressmen so badly that they scurried across the
river to Princeton, where they took refuge, sheeplike, in the
college.

Nor did the Congress command any more respect than this
abroad. Theoretically it was authorized to treat for the thirteen

states with foreign nations, but in practice it could not promise anything, for it couldn't command—it could only recommend, which recommendations the several states acted upon or not, as they saw fit. When a peace was being patched up in Paris to put an end to the Revolution, the British, tired, in despair, gave way on point after point; but there was one thing that they did insist upon—that the loyalists whose property had been seized in America be given at least some sort of opportunity to sue for that property to be returned. Even this the delegates from America could not promise. They could speak for the Continental Congress, but the Continental Congress could not speak for the states. What finally happened was that Great Britain gave in, accepting Congress's assurance that it would strongly *advise* the states to adopt such a policy. This it did; and not one state paid any attention. What foreign power in its right mind would seek to do business with a hands-tied organization like that?

The Continental Congress had little to do with the people as such, for it was answerable only to the states. Its members were not directly elected: they were named by the sundry legislatures, which could at any time remove them. The delegations invariably voted as units, and if one was evenly split— and there was nothing to control the size of a delegation and no restrictions on absenteeism—then its vote was cast out.

Moreover, for all practical purposes the Continental Congress did not contain within itself any means of making itself better, for the Articles of Confederation under which it existed provided that they could be revised or amended only by unanimous vote of all thirteen states, which was unthinkable.

If the political affairs of the United States were rapidly approaching a state of anarchy, the financial affairs were already there.

No national currency, paper or metal, was in existence. There was no set standard. Many thought in terms of pounds, shillings, pence, and these were the means of exchange in dealings with Great Britain, but even these values varied from place to place, and the Spanish dollar, the commonest unit,[3] was

EXAMPLES OF CONTINENTAL BILLS

worth six shillings in New England, eight shillings in New York, seven shillings sixpence in Pennsylvania, thirty-two shillings sixpence in South Carolina, and so forth. This would have been bad enough, but there were all sorts of other coins in circulation—carolins, guineas, English crowns, French crowns, moidores, pistareens, doubloons, ducats, Johannes, half joes, to name but a few—and not only was there a great deal of chipping, there was a great deal of out-and-out counterfeiting. Every merchant had a tested set of scales, which he used all the time in his shop and took with him when he had to go out for orders or deliveries. This was particularly hard on travelers, who if they were not similarly equipped might be shortchanged by as much as twenty per cent.

Business was bad along the coast, now that America no longer was protected by the Mother Country—the Nantucket whaling fleet had shrunk from 150 sail before the Revolution to 19 afterward, to name but one item—and it was even worse inland, the farmers being the hardest hit. Some ninety per cent of the population were farmers, too.

Hostilities were ended in 1781, with the surrender of Cornwallis's army at Yorktown, but there was no formal peace until 1783. By that time there was hardship at home. The new republic was not even rich in land then, for the western territories were still under dispute, and it had no cash at all. The soldiers, unpaid, glowered; while civilians asked to know why there should *be* any soldiers, now that the war was over. After the shortages of the war years there was a human desire to get a few luxuries again, but these had to be paid for, for the English merchants—and the goods came mostly from England —were not inclined to extend much tick to such an unstable buyer. Debts mounted. Creditors, with a terrible machinery at their command, scowled.

A cry for paper currency was inevitable. Get the printing presses to work! It was perfectly simple. There wasn't enough money, so why shouldn't the states make some? They had that sovereign right, didn't they?

Many succumbed, almost half of them; and in the others there were strong paper-money parties. The result was even more debt, and the withdrawal, in accordance with Gresham's Law, of much of the good money.

New York, amid much snarling, put a heavy duty on farm products from New Jersey on one side and Connecticut on the other, at the same time affixing an export fee upon goods shipped through the port of New York to those states, which, naturally, squealed.

There were riots in Pennsylvania and even in conservative New Hampshire, and threats of riots in many other places, for the paper-money people pushed hard.

Until the outbreak of Shays' Rebellion, however, Rhode Island had been the worst. "Rogues' Island," as exasperated neighbors called it, had been founded for the "otherwise-minded," not to say cranks; and this tradition survived. The smallest state went in for inflation in a very big way. To protect its all-but-worthless money it issued all sorts of constraining writs—called "Know-ye's" from their opening words—against all sorts of persons, fairly flooding the state with them. The usual pattern of creditor chasing debtor was reversed when the Rhode Island creditors, not wishing to be paid in Rhode Island notes, hid. Shops were closed. The farmers refused to take their products into town, where they would be paid with "shin plasters," and this intensified the old antagonism between country and city. Commerce was at a standstill. Everything that could possibly go wrong, it seemed, went wrong.

It was Shays' Rebellion, however, that really capped the climax, and caused thoughtful men all over the country to sit up sharp, popping their eyes. One of the most profoundly shocked of these men was the master of Mount Vernon, who, as he himself put it, felt as if he were in a dream—a nightmare, no doubt. "God only knows what the result will be," he wrote to a friend. General Knox, a faithful correspondent, kept him acquainted with events from the field, and Knox was alarmed at the behavior of the rebels, those "desperate and unprincipled men" who were chiefly of "the young and active part of the community" and who were "determined to annihilate all debts public and private."

Washington was in a delicate position just at that time, and the news of the doings in western Massachusetts caused him to make a decision at least as momentous as any he had ever made on the field of battle.

This man was not coy. When he said, on retiring to Mount Vernon, that he was done with public life, he meant it. He was himself in debt, as were all the planters; and he had a heap of work to do.

Aside from his correspondence, which was voluminous, his only outside concern was with the Potomac Company, of which he was president. Washington always had been intensely interested in the development of the lands west of the mountains; and now that Spain, which controlled the mouth of the Mississippi, was threatening to shut all navigation on that river to the

GEORGE WASHINGTON

western American colonists, it seemed a good time for him to do something about his long-time dream of opening up the Potomac, the "River of Swans," between Fort Cumberland and Great Falls, which would in effect join the east and west. Even to start on such a grandiose project it would be necessary to gain the co-operation of the other side of the river—namely, Maryland. That state was politely invited, and as politely accepted, and there was a conference at Alexandria which soon adjourned to Mount Vernon. It was agreed that the project was too big for two states and that others should be asked in, say Delaware and Pennsylvania. Then somebody suggested that while they were at it why didn't they invite *all* of the states and make it a convention on not only the Potomac plan but on all the ills and misfittings and shortcomings that bedeviled them; and this was done, the convention being called to sit at Annapolis the first Monday in September, 1786.

Five of the states appointed delegates who attended this convention, four appointed delegates who didn't take the trouble to attend, and four did not even appoint any delegates. It was not an encouraging start. Yet there was a feeling at the convention, such as it was, that at least a beginning *had* been made; and it was agreed to call another and a larger convention, with more preparation, at Philadelphia on May 14, 1787, "to take into consideration the situation of the United States, to devise such further provisions as shall appear to them necessary to render the constitution of the federal government adequate to the exigencies of the Union; and to report such an act for that purpose to the United States in Congress assembled, as, when agreed to by them, and afterwards confirmed by the legislature of every state, will effectually provide for the same." A large order.

Copies of the resolution, which had been framed by a young lawyer from New York named Alexander Hamilton, were sent to each state legislature, and then, as though by afterthought, to Congress.

Congress hesitated for a long while, and at last, February 21, 1787, without even mentioning the notice it had received, it called its *own* convention in that same place at that same time, a convention, it was careful to add, "for the sole and express purpose of revising the articles of confederation."

This was when Washington got into his dilemma. He had not attended the Annapolis convention, but from the beginning he was coaxed by close friends to go to the convention at Philadelphia, which, it was argued, would be a failure without him. He didn't want to go. His rheumatism was annoying him from time to time, his mother and sister were seriously ill, and there were many matters at Mount Vernon that needed his personal attention. He had cited these reasons for turning down an invitation to preside at the annual meeting of the Society of the Cincinnati which was to be held in Philadelphia the same month as the convention, May. How would it look if he was found in that city at the same time? He had vowed that he was through with public life, but what could be more public than a convention, especially as, if he went, they would almost certainly name him the presiding officer?

He demurred. He did not flatly refuse, but he hemmed and hawed (which was not like him) and gave the impression that he wouldn't go. His great fear was that the convention would be a resounding failure, making him look foolish for having attended, wounding his prestige, which just then could hardly have been higher, could move only down. Some states, he believed, would not appoint delegates, while some delegates, appointed, would not attend: clearly he had in mind the Annapolis convention, to which he had *not* gone. Moreover, the delegates might be inferior men, petty politicians whom his own august presence would tend further to belittle. Should he give countenance to such a gathering? He thought not. Look at his own Virginia. Patrick Henry, the most persuasive voice in the Old Dominion, had been appointed a delegate, but had refused to serve, saying that he "smelt a rat." Thomas Nelson, Jr., another powerful figure, likewise abstained. Richard Henry Lee pleaded, none too convincingly, ill health.

Yet Governor Randolph and James Madison, close friends, continued to press Washington, and as he wavered there came the news of more and more states appointing big-name delegates.

It was his duty, Madison and Randolph said.

George Washington was never a man to shirk his duty to his country. He assented; and from that moment it was at least sure that the convention would be taken seriously.

Chapter 3

One by One

THE FIRST to arrive, eleven days early, was James Madison. He was a slight man, slim and trim, five feet six, who walked with a bouncy step, as though the ground beneath him was pneumatic. Sometimes called "the non-oratorical Virginian," he had a high reedy voice and always talked as though he had just at that moment thought of what he was saying, though in truth nineteen times out of twenty the speech had been prepared. He had blue eyes and tawny hair that was receding in front, though he was only thirty-five. At Princeton (class of '71) he had been known as a lover of dirty stories and bawdy songs, but in adult life he was seriousness personified, very proper in speech as in dress. He never used a curse word, for example, and had no truck with those new double-breasted coats.

He came to Philadelphia not from his native state but from New York, where he had been attending a session of the Continental Congress. He had read everything about confederacies that he could lay hands on, from ancient Greece to eighteenth-century Europe, and he had strong ideas as to what the United States needed—a powerful central government, with the states decidedly secondary—but he was much too clever to shout this at his fellow delegates. He would *talk* it to them, quietly but almost pauselessly, being always ready to answer a question. He was the best-prepared man at that convention. He had asked the other Virginia delegates to get to Philadelphia early, so that they could be ready with a definite plan, drawn up in advance, something that he sensed no other state would have. George

JAMES MADISON

Wythe and John Blair at least obeyed him, arriving only a few days after Madison, and this gave the delegation a quorum, for the Virginia legislature had stipulated that as few as three out of the seven appointed delegates could cast the vote of that state. Preliminary conferences began right away, with James Madison doing virtually all of the talking.

He had taken up residence at the town's best-known boarding house, that of Mrs. Mary House, at Fifth and Market. When Washington arrived in Philadelphia, Sunday, May 13, one day before the convention was scheduled to begin, he was met at the city line by an honor guard, which, to the booming of salutatory cannons, started to escort him to this same Widow

House's house, where he planned to put up; but his friend Robert Morris, the man who almost single-handedly had financed the Revolution, talked him into being his guest at the fine old three-story brick mansion in Market Street near Sixth Street, a landmark. This had been the property of Robert Penn when he was the proprietory governor of Pennsylvania, and in the Revolution it had served as headquarters for Sir William Howe and later for Major General Benedict Arnold when these two were in turn the military governors of Philadelphia. Now Morris owned it.

Washington's first act was to pay a courtesy call on Benjamin Franklin, governor in effect of Pennsylvania and head of that state's large and strong delegation to the Constitutional Convention. At eighty-one years Franklin would be, easily, the oldest delegate. He could not be described as spry, for he suffered from gout and the stone and on bad days would not venture out of his house on Market Street near Fourth, or even into the pleasant garden there "with grass plots and gravel walks, with trees and flowering shrubs," and with, too, an already famous mulberry tree under which in fine weather the sage loved to sit and receive his friends. But his mind was as keen as ever, and he could still tell an outrageous story with the old twinkle in his eyes, and still liked to be surrounded by pretty women, and still, too, when he could, liked to sit up through the night over one or two or even three bottles. Every distinguished visitor to Philadelphia called on Ben Franklin. It was a custom.

Next morning they assembled at the State House in the same room in which the Declaration of Independence had been adopted and signed. There was nothing for them to do except exchange civilities. There was not anything like a quorum. Four of the seven Virginians were present, to be sure, and probably all of the eight Pennsylvania delegates, since these were all residents of Philadelphia—the state Supreme Executive Council had ordered that four of the Pennsylvania delegates would constitute a quorum for that delegation—but there was nobody else.

Independence Hall
Philadelphia · Built 1732

INDEPENDENCE HALL, PHILADELPHIA

It didn't embarrass them. They were not in a hurry.

There were two Morrises in the Pennsylvania delegation—the largest—but they were not related, and side by side they made up a dramatic contrast. Robert Morris, the financier, Washington's host, was a thoughtful man of business, middle-aged, taciturn: At the Constitutional Convention he seldom opened his mouth. The other Morris, Gouverneur, seldom *closed* his. He was verbose, he was exuberant, he was thirty-five, this high-liver, this butterfly among the dogged moths. He could almost be called a professional bachelor, and though cer-

GOUVERNEUR MORRIS

tainly not a professional politician, he was skillful, resourceful, and hard-working. He could see no reason why a patriot shouldn't laugh now and then; and if certain of the old-timers, such as that slightly besmudged corsetmaker-turned-propagandist Tom Paine and the dour, disagreeable John Adams, tut-tutted and shook their heads when Gouverneur Morris's name was spoken, others, like John Jay, a lean, accipitrine man of Huguenot ancestry, and George Washington himself, who could be scarcely be classed among the frivolous, disapproved of many of Gouverneur Morris's pastimes but loved him all the same.

A gentleman to his fingertips, this Morris did not stoop to the gentlemanly weaknesses of his time. He set a good table and kept a good cellar, but never drank himself under the table. Tobacco and snuff he thought disgusting. As for the gambling that was rampant in high circles, he simply could not see any sense to it. He had inherited a little money, and made more. He had all he needed, and derived no thrill from risking it. At most he would play for small stakes just to be sociable, but he gave all his gains to the servants. However, show this man a beautiful lady—and he was lost. She had to *be* a lady! Gouverneur Morris was no Casanova, no Boswell, to be diverted by a serving wench when nothing more highborn chanced to be at hand. But set him before some incandescent duchess, or before some countess who might well prove less unapproachable than her hoop-petticoats caused her to appear, and he went to work right away. He was indefatigable. He must have heard many "no's," but he had a lot of fun. He was a tall man with broad shoulders and a grand masculine build—the French sculptor Houdon got him to pose for a figure of Washington, doing only the head, later, from life—but he had a wooden leg, his left. This was the result of a carriage accident, and though he never pretended that it was anything else, in popular rumor it had been caused by a jump from the window of a lady's bedroom—with an enraged husband in close pursuit. If Gouverneur Morris himself ever heard this story—and it is possible that he did, for he got around a good deal—he must have been vastly amused.

There was another telling member of the Pennsylvania delegation, a man less ingratiating but by no means less effective in parliamentary debate. This was James Wilson, a burly, surly Scot, an accomplished classical scholar who had come to this country twenty years before to teach. He had studied law here, and he became highly successful at the bar. He had been a member of Congress for many years, and was a Signer of the Declaration of Independence. Like Madison he believed in a strong central government, and like Madison again he got his effects less through oratory—though Wilson, unlike Madison, was a good public speaker—than through watchfulness, preparation, resourcefulness, and plain ordinary fight. They seemed never to tire, those two, never to flag. Wilson had a slight but discernible burr in his speech, and he sometimes wore steel-rimmed spectacles, so that when he shook a stumpy forefinger at his fellow delegates he looked for all the world like what a little earlier he had in fact been, a schoolteacher. He was not attractive, and not eminently quotable, but he was one of the giants.

So the Virginians and Pennsylvanians passed the time of day in that beautiful high-ceilinged, white-paneled chamber, and they agreed to meet at eleven o'clock the next morning, same place. None of them was worried. After all, much depended upon the weather, the roads. It could take two weeks to ride from New Hampshire to Philadelphia. It could take *three* weeks from Georgia. They drifted out.

Next day two more Virginians arrived, Edmund Randolph and James McClurg. McClurg, who had been a Virginia militia surgeon during the Revolution, had taken his M.D. at the University of Edinburgh, for like Wilson of Pennsylvania he was a Scotsman born. Madison had personally picked him when Patrick Henry declined to serve, and Madison knew that he would vote right. Madison was not so sure of Randolph, who at thirty-four was governor of the state. Randolph was a fine, large, handsome man, well acquainted with the give and take of political debate, utterly sincere, a patriot, but not yet sure of what he sought by coming to Philadelphia. He could see, and had seen for some time, that changes in the current setup were needed, but he was inclined to think that the task could be done by patching up the Articles of Confederation. Madison, who had been working on him for some time back at home, renewed this work in Philadelphia. But he had to do it carefully. You didn't push Edmund Randolph around.

The next day there came from the south the last of the Virginia delegates, George Mason, a quiet, distinguished, studious man who had framed the Virginia Declaration of Rights, the document upon which Jefferson leaned so heavily when he wrote the Declaration of Independence.

At the same time there came down from New York, where they had been attending Congress, two South Carolina delegates, the venerable John Rutledge, and Charles Pinckney, an energetic opinionated young man who was sometimes called "Me-too Charlie" by those who did not like him.

It had been agreed, without any formal vote—how could there have been a formal vote?—that when seven states had quorums present the convention would start.

Friday the eighteenth two-thirds of the New York delegation showed up. This was a curious one. The governor of New York, George Clinton, was known to be against a strong central government, a federal government. True, as much could have been said of almost any state governor, Randolph of Virginia excepted, for they feared the loss of their local importance; but in the case of New York, Clinton's grip on the political machinery was so firm that there were many in Philadelphia who expressed astonishment—and pleasure—that this state had condescended to send a delegation at all.

Standing out in this delegation was one of Governor Clinton's bitterest enemies, the almost blatantly brilliant Alexander Hamilton, a successful lawyer of thirty-two who was known to be fervently in favor of a strong federal government and was rumored to be even in favor of some sort of king, for he was markedly aristocratic in his ways. Hamilton was liked by few, if any, but he was feared by most. He was no great shakes as an orator, but he could be very persuasive in personal talk and was an expert practitioner of what was then called "out-of-door" work—that is, the off-the-floor buttonholing of fellow delegates, low, intense, telling talk.[4]

Paired with Hamilton, as though to make sure that he never had a chance to cast New York's vote as he would have wished, were two loyal Clinton men, Robert Yates, a justice of the state Supreme Court, and stammering John Lansing, the young mayor of Albany. Only Yates was with Hamilton in person on the eighteenth. Lansing was still on his way.

These two, Lansing and Yates, stood for everything that Alexander Hamilton opposed, and they would be sure to vote against him every time there was a division. New York, like South Carolina, like Georgia, required two for a quorum. Even if one of the opposing pair was absent, from sickness or another cause, the remaining one's voice would offset that of Hamilton, and both would thereupon be thrown out. Clinton couldn't lose.

On Monday, May 21, small, weak-eyed George Read, the ardent Methodist Richard Bassett, and that taciturn Quaker Jacob Broom[5] appeared from Delaware, a state that, like Virginia, called for a quorum of three.

But—where was New England?

The following day there were some additional southerners: former Governor Alexander Martin, Richard D. Spaight, William Richardson Davie, and Hugh Williamson, all from North Carolina, which state called for a quorum of three.

On the twenty-fourth there came the rest of the imposing South Carolina delegation: Charles Cotesworth Pinckney, a brigadier general and second cousin to "Me-too Charlie," and Pierce Butler, a planter.

Also present, having come from New York and the Congress, were William Few of Georgia and Rufus King of Massachusetts, the first New England man to show his face. King was young and impressionable, and Alexander Hamilton, who singled him out for a long, low, earnest talk, caused him completely to change his mind about the need for a central government. King would vote Hamilton's way, he agreed.

New Jersey was right across the river from Philadelphia, but it was not until May 25, eleven days after the convention was supposed to have started, that the New Jersey delegation hove into sight—David Brearley, chief justice of the state, William Paterson, the former attorney general, and William Churchill Houston, a professor of mathematics at Princeton.

This made seven states, complete.

The members of the convention thereupon posted guards at the door, and they sat down and declared themselves to be in session.

It was a raw chilly day, with much rain.

Chapter 4

The Real Work Begins

THE ILLEGITIMATE SON of an illegitimate father, William Temple Franklin, put in a bid for the clerkship of the convention, but despite his illustrious grandfather, who because of the weather was not present, he lost to Major William Jackson, a former assistant secretary of war.

The unofficial clerk—and a much more efficient one—was James Madison, a delegate, who the very first session posted himself in the center, up near the president's chair, and maintained this place throughout, hearing everything, making copious notes, which later he would write out in full. There were others who took notes from time to time—Yates, Major Pierce of Georgia, Paterson of New Jersey, Hamilton, Pinckney the younger, Rufus King, McHenry of Maryland, Mason—but the whole bunch put together made up no such mine of information as Madison was to provide. Moreover, while he kept busy in this way Madison never missed a trick on the floor, and would be on his feet instantly when some pet project of his was threatened.

Though Benjamin Franklin was not physically present, his words were there. He had written them out; and the ordinarily clamlike Robert Morris read them for him. It astounded no one that the speech nominated George Washington for chairman or president of the convention. Rutledge of South Carolina, the second oldest delegate present, seconded the nomination. In all seriousness they took the vote by means of paper ballots, and it turned out to be unanimous. The Mount Vernon planter was escorted to the chair by Morris and Rutledge. This chair was

36

on a dais behind the desk on which the Declaration of Independence had been signed, and it had been occupied by successive presidents of the Second Continental Congress. There was a rising sun, or perhaps a setting sun, carved on its back. Washington filled it well. Even in that small hall his words were sometimes almost inaudible, because of the trouble that he had with his badly fitted wooden teeth; but he didn't say much anyway, and he *looked* magnificent there.

GEORGE WASHINGTON ADDRESSING THE
CONSTITUTIONAL CONVENTION

He started the proceedings by making a short, simple, apologetic speech of thanks for this honor, of which he declared himself unworthy. No doubt he meant this. The man had no wile. He said that he had never occupied such a chair before, and he hoped that if he erred through ignorance and inexperience they would forgive him. Then he sat down; and thereafter he spoke only when he had to.

The clerk's first business was to examine the credentials of the various delegations, and right away the population issue, the big-states-versus-small-states clash, cast its shadow upon the convention. It was generally known that the Virginians had concocted a plan that they would place before the convention, and it was believed—correctly, as it turned out—that this plan provided for representation in the central ruling body, whatever that might be, by population rather than equally among the various states. The little states did not like this.

The Virginia Plan was to stipulate that either population or the amount of wealth a state had—the sum that it could be called upon to pay into the central body—would be the measure of its representation. Now, property was awkward to assess. What was worth much in one place was worth little in another. The South counted a good part of its wealth in slaves, of which the North had few. Time too might make a difference—good times here, not good times just then in another place. Heads, however, were easily counted. So it was understood, almost from the beginning, that what was meant was population.

Virginia was the biggest state that way, having almost 750,000 people. Pennsylvania—the delegates of which were rumored to be backing the so-called Virginia Plan—was third, with about 430,000, which meant that it was as populous as Rhode Island, New Hampshire, New Jersey, Delaware, and Georgia, all rolled into one. Massachusetts was second, and North Carolina and New York were fourth and fifth respectively.

Not even the Virginia credentials instructed the delegates to propose a brand-new constitution, the abolishment rather than the amendment of the Articles of Confederation. Most of the instructions from other states charged the delegates with studying and perhaps altering the Articles. Those of the Delaware delegation stated emphatically that there was to be no voting-by-population in the federal governing body. There were 60,000 residents of Delaware, the smallest state represented —Rhode Island had already announced that she was not interested—and since according to the Articles of Confederation an amendment must be passed unanimously by all thirteen states, those 60,000 might conceivably balk the purpose of all the rest of the nation.

A committee—Wythe of Virginia, Hamilton of New York,

Charles Pinckney of South Carolina—was appointed to frame a set of rules to regulate future meetings.

A doorman and a messenger were appointed, without opposition.

The meeting was then adjourned until Monday, May 28, at eleven o'clock in the morning.

The next day, Saturday, was spent in informal discussions, especially at the Indian Queen, a coffee house and inn on Fourth Street between Market and Chestnut, where many of the delegates had rooms.

Sunday there was an unconventional diversion. Pennsylvania was a liberal state and in certain circumstances would even permit Roman Catholics to worship, and there was such a church right there in Philadelphia. To the Pennsylvanians themselves it was no novelty, but the Virginians, the week before, had gone to its service as a matter of immense curiosity, though without George Washington (who had pressing social duties, as the poor man always did have). Many of the other delegates, on this Sunday, May 27, attended mass, and this time Washington was among them. It was very interesting, the sort of thing that ordinarily they would never have had a chance to see and hear. "I was struck with solemnity of the apparatus," George Mason wrote to his son, "and could not help remarking how much everything was calculated to warm the imagination and captivate the senses. No wonder that this should be the popular religion of Europe! The church music was exceedingly fine, but while I was pleased with the air of solemnity so generally diffused thro the Church, I was somewhat disgusted with the frequent tinckling of a little bell; which put me in mind of the drawing up of the curtain for a puppet show. I wonder they have not substituted some more solemn and deep toned instrument."

Washington, in a spare moment, wrote back to his caretaker at Mount Vernon, asking how the buckwheat was coming. Buckwheat was a new crop for him, and he was worried about it.

Monday morning a reassuring fan of new faces was in the

State House, all eager to be at the deliberations. There were Nathaniel Gorham and Caleb Strong from Massachusetts, who with Rufus King made up the quorum from that state. There was Oliver Ellsworth, with assurance that a couple of others would soon appear from Connecticut. There was Gunning Bedford, a man of mighty girth, from Delaware. There was James McHenry of Maryland.[6] And certain Pennsylvanians who had not attended the first real meeting, three days before, came now —Franklin himself, Thomas Mifflin, George Clymer, Jared Ingersoll.

The report of the rules committee was received and read twice—once by Wythe, again by the clerk. It contained nothing startling, though clearly it had been well pondered. A couple of minor items were rejected, but on the really important clause —that the authorized delegates from seven states would make up a quorum—there was no dispute.

Spaight of North Carolina proposed that it be the intent of the convention that if a resolution was voted for, that resolution did not thereupon become irrevocable. In other words, he pointed out, the convention should be entitled to reconsider, perhaps to change its mind. This, as it happened, was an excellent idea. It was applauded.

Pierce Butler of South Carolina put out another important proposal: that the press be rigorously excluded from all the doings of the convention, which the members themselves should agree would be kept absolutely secret. This too was agreed upon.[7]

Dinner would be at four o'clock in the afternoon. As that hour approached work was suspended until eleven the following morning.

There was one last-minute item. A letter from certain unauthorized but noteworthy residents of Rhode Island was laid on the table. It expressed regret that Rhode Island would not attend the convention officially, since the upper house of its governing body would not go along with the lower house, but the letter added that it was hoped that the convention would not, for that reason, discriminate against Rhode Island. This was accepted without comment.

And so the Constitutional Convention ended its first full day of business.

Next morning there were two new faces, those of John Dickinson of Delaware, an austere, rather prosy, rather pompous personage, and Elbridge Gerry of Massachusetts, a waspish, fussy, voluble little man. Each of these was to have a lot to say.

The first order of business was the strengthening and formalizing of the Spaight and Butler suggestions of the previous day, suggestions that the delegates found good.

The Spaight proposal, after a little discussion, came out as this resolution: "That a motion to reconsider a matter which has been determined by a majority, may be made with leave unanimously given, on the same day on which the vote passed; but otherwise not without one day's previous notice, in which last case, if the House agree to the reconsideration, some future day shall be assigned for that purpose."

This worked out well. The delegates were feeling their way, as they knew. They were doing something they never had done before; and a slip now and then, a stumble, was to be expected. They were not dogmatic.

This attitude accounted too for the formalizing of the Butler suggestion, the secrecy resolution, in which they not only determined to forbid the outside publication of any journal or notes of the convention but also pledged themselves not to discuss the proceedings beyond the State House.

This resolution was criticized adversely later by men who were not there at the time, but none of the delegates at the opening sessions showed any wariness of it, and even the press, which might have been expected to poniard such a stand, on the whole nodded approval. There would be differences, naturally; and if the differences were aired at the time, the end product, if there was to be an end product, would hardly inspire confidence in the public that must pass upon it.

The secrecy did, of course, give rise to frenetic rumors,

both in America and in Europe, but especially in Europe, where the consensus was that the convention would come up with some manner of monarchy. A republic, it was argued, could not survive in such a large territory. Venice, yes; Switzerland, yes; but not a sprawl of states like America. The king system would once again be resorted to, surely; and Europe always had a few potential kings to spare. There was even betting on which sprig of royalty would be asked to take over. It was confidentially reported that Prince Henry of Prussia had been approached, and also Frederick Augustus, Duke of York and Bishop of Osnabrück, second son of George III (this was before the Bishop created a great scandal in high circles by permitting his mistress to get rich by selling commissions in the British Army, of which the Bishop somewhat unaccountably was the head).[8] There were those in America who believed such stories too; but the delegates had nothing to say—out of doors.

On the floor they had a great deal to say, as James Madison's busy pen attested. On this same day, Tuesday, May 29, Governor Randolph presented to the convention the so-called Virginia Plan, a set of fifteen resolutions; and the delegates really got down to work.

Randolph had praise for the Articles of Confederation and for their framers, whom he described as "wise and great men" (four of them were listening to him: Elbridge Gerry, John Dickinson, Gouverneur Morris, and Robert Morris). But, he added, the Articles were adopted in war times, under stress. They were no longer adequate. Something more stable was called for, something that had been thoroughly thought out. He reviewed the whole situation, the state of near-anarchy that prevailed through the country, and before submitting the Virginia resolutions he made it clear, in the convention's first full-length speech, that these were not meant to be rigid, a set system, but merely suggestions, which could be changed as the members thought best. Virginia was not irretrievably committed to them. The convention should discuss them thoroughly.

This the convention most certainly did.

Chapter 5

A Big Day

THE CONVENTION started the very next morning to take up the
Virginia Plan step by step; and it was at once apparent that this
would prove to be a very long process.

The Committee of the Whole device was used for the preliminary discussions. This is a sometimes useful, if seemingly
silly, piece of parliamentary machinery, by means of which the
sitting body simply declares itself to be a committee, and that
committee, though consisting of the very same members as the
parent body, debates the issue *as* a committee. In time, when it
has reached a decision, it reports back to itself. The Committee
of the Whole permits a great deal of off-the-record talk and
allows a man to change his mind and even his vote at any time
before the final report, without being written down for posterity as a shuttlecock. To be sure, the formalized Spaight resolution of the previous day did the same thing; but the delegates,
conscious that they were undertaking a unique task, aware of
their own shortcomings, were playing it safe.

A Massachusetts judge, Nathaniel Gorham, a new face at
the convention, was elected chairman of the Committee of the
Whole. The hour of assembling was set ahead to ten o'clock, so
that the members could get to their eating places in time for
four o'clock dinner; and there was no lunch break. Every morning, then, the convention carefully declared itself to be sitting
as a Committee of the Whole, and George Washington stepped
down from the chairman's place, which then was occupied by
Judge Gorham, a man much more experienced in this line of

work, and a few minutes before 4:00 P.M. the Committee of the Whole declared itself to be back in session as a convention, the two men changed places again, and Washington from the dais adjourned the convention until the following morning.

Thus relegated to the floor, George Washington was an attentive delegate. He never made a speech, but he listened to the other speeches and he always voted in his own delegation.

To the first of the Virginia resolutions there could hardly have been any objection. It read:

"1. Resolved, That the articles of Confederation ought to be so corrected and enlarged as to accomplish the objects proposed by their institution; namely, common defence, security of liberty and general welfare."

EDMUND RANDOLPH

Randolph, however, proposed that before they took up the resolutions one by one they pass upon three more precise substitute ones, so that they would better know where they stood. The first two of these were somewhat vague, and the Committee of the Whole passed them without a vote, without comment. The third made members sit up in their seats:

"Resolved, That a National Government ought to be established consisting of a supreme Legislative, Executive and Judiciary."

That stunned them; and for several minutes there was silence. Then the questions started. What was the exact meaning of that word "national," the word that so frightened them? Nobody seemed to know. What was the difference, if there was one, between "national" and "federal"? Did this resolution mean that the sundry state governments would be replaced altogether? Randolph said it only meant that the national government would have such powers as the various state governments by name ceded to it. There were doubters from the South and from New England, but the Pennsylvania and Virginia men had planned this thing well. A strong central government now or a despot within twenty years—take your choice, Gouverneur Morris told the delegates. And George Mason lent the weight of his prestige to the resolution as well.

In the end it prevailed. New York was divided, and so it could not vote, Hamilton being for, Yates against. New Jersey did not happen to have a quorum that day. Connecticut, which allowed one delegate to speak for it, was represented by a newcomer, Roger Sherman, a dry, cautious, nasal ex-shoemaker—the southern members had difficulty in understanding his Yankee drawl—who had signed the Articles of Association, the Declaration of Independence, and the Articles of Confederation. He voted no. But he sat alone. Delaware, Virginia, the two Carolinas, Pennsylvania, and Massachusetts voted for the resolution.

The delegates had taken a giant step. It frightened them a little, so early in the proceedings. They had voted, in effect, to scrap the Articles of Confederation and to devise something to put into their place. They were virtually committed, now, to a constitution.

The next two Virginia resolutions, as first read to the assembly, were:

"2. Resolved, therefore, That the rights of suffrage in the National Legislature ought to be proportioned to the Quotas of contribution, or to the number of free inhabitants, as the one or the other rule may seem best in different cases.

"3. Resolved, That the National Legislature ought to consist of two branches."

When the time came for discussion of these Edmund Randolph proposed that Number 3 be taken up first. He knew that he was due for a fierce battle on Number 2. A serious fight this early in the convention might break it up. Wait until they got used to one another before they started to squabble. The delegates from Delaware, indeed, were ready to walk out then and there, for they said that their instructions forbade them to vote for any changes that involved representation in proportion to population, and they were only coaxed into staying by the implied promise that the whole matter could be talked over at length later.

To the matter of a bicameral legislature there was no real opposition. Franklin (who was feeling better) was known to favor one house, as his own state of Pennsylvania had it, but he didn't care enough to make a fuss. Sherman did put in the observation that the current Congress had been criticized not because it lacked an extra house but because it lacked power; but he too didn't really care.

Still discreetly sidestepping Number 2, the session then took up the first part of Number 4, which provided that members of the "first branch of the National Legislature" should be elected directly by the people. Here was a startling suggestion, put forward by the aristocratical Virginians, promptly opposed by town-meeting New Englanders. Gerry and Sherman croaked that the people were chronically ill-informed, misled, the dupes of so-called patriots who in fact were mere demagogues. Mason demurred. The first branch, he said, should be "the grand depository of the democratic principles of the Government." They should attend to the rights "of every class of people," he insisted. Wilson backed this. Gerry said no. In his opinion—and he was no doubt thinking of Shays' Rebellion—"the evils we experience flow from the excess of democracy." The other members of his delegation seemingly did not agree with him, for when the division came Massachusetts voted "aye," as did North Carolina, Georgia, Virginia, Pennsylvania, and New York. New Jersey and South Carolina voted no. Connecticut and Delaware were split. The clause was declared carried, then, by 6 to 2.

Thus in the first vote that called for a choice between the popular public will and the judgment of selected office holders, the populars won. The opposition, however, had only been shushed, not silenced. There was still a great deal of feeling in favor of having members of the first branch —"first branch" and "second branch" were always used, no other names—elected by the several state legislatures. This was to come up again.

Number 5 would have provided that the second branch of the national legislature be elected by the first branch "out of a proper number of persons nominated by the individual Legislatures," but this too would be a contentious one, what with the Delaware delegates clamoring for their one-state-one-vote system. It was avoided, though not without a vote, which struck it down; but the question had not been fought through.

The convention then took up Number 6: "Resolved, That each branch ought to possess the right of originating Acts; that the National Legislature ought to be impowered to enjoy the Legislature Rights vested in Congress by the Confederation, and moreover to legislate in all cases to which the separate States are incompetent, or in which the harmony of the United States may be interrupted by the exercise of individual Legislation; to negative all laws passed by the several States, contravening in the opinion of the National Legislature the several articles of Union; and to call forth the force of the Union against any member of the Union failing to fulfil its duties under the articles thereof."

Here was a large order. To the first clause, permitting

either "branch" to originate legislation, there was no objection. The second wasn't clear, South Carolinians complained. What was meant by "incompetent"? Weren't these powers exceedingly broad? Wouldn't it be better to *enumerate* the powers that were about to be given to a national legislature? Randolph said that he had no thought of giving such a body sweeping, unlimited powers. Madison said he thought that enumeration of powers would be fine theoretically but practically too difficult. The clause was adopted, the vote being unanimous excepting for Connecticut, which was split, Ellsworth aye, Sherman nay. But there must have been many mental reservations, and few doubted that the matter would be brought up in debate once more.

The same thing applies to the next clause, the "to negative" clause. (The noun "veto" or the verb "to veto" never were used in the debates or in any of the ensuing documents: it was always "negative.") This was Madison's own idea, and it was designed to keep the states from passing all sorts of offensive, retaliatory laws against one another, a practice that was one of the compelling reasons for this convention. Some sort of control over state legislation there must be, but there were those who thought that this ought to be given to the executive, a department that had not yet even been discussed. Nobody mentioned the judicial department. The clause was accepted, but only temporarily.

The last clause in this resolution, again, would need a great deal more discussion than they could afford to give it today—for it was almost dinnertime. Madison himself admitted that he had his doubts about it. "A union of the States containing such an ingredient seems to provide for its own destruction. The use of force against a State would look more like a declaration of war than an infliction of punishment; and would probably be considered by the party attacked as a dissolution of all previous compacts by which it might be bound." He moved that consideration of this clause be postponed, and that motion was agreed to, *nem. con.*, which is to say nobody contradicting.

Then the two chairmen changed seats again, and the convention called it a day—a big day.

Chapter 6

Unanimity Hall

THE GEORGIA DELEGATION was now complete, three men. William Few had come early from Congress in New York, and on the day when the debate on the Virginia Plan really got under way, the last day of May, William Pierce appeared from that same place. The following day William Houstoun arrived from Georgia itself.

These were not brilliant men, and they had little to say for themselves, but one, Major Pierce, has been the delight of historians because of the notes he took. Not only did he epitomize speeches; he gave thumbnail sketches of the other delegates—how they looked, how they spoke.

On the whole, he was favorably impressed by the others, but the standard of oratory disappointed him. Rufus King he found "much distinguished for his eloquence and great parliamentary talents," and Gouverneur Morris fascinated him, for "He winds through all the mazes of Rhetoric, and throws around him such a glare that he charms, captivates, and leads away the senses of all who hear him. . . . But with all these powers he is fickle and inconstant,—never pursuing one train of thinking,—nor ever regular."

These were exceptions. Major Pierce was a southern gentleman, who liked his speech-making florid, in the spread-eagle tradition. Repeatedly in his precious little pen portraits he complains of the lack of this. Thus, Gerry was "without respect to eloquence or flower of diction"; "as a Speaker he (Caleb Strong) is feeble, and without confidence"; while of Dr. Johnson of

Connecticut he thought that "As an Orator in my opinion, there is nothing in him that warrants the high reputation which he has for public speaking." Alexander Hamilton awed him as a person, but not as a speaker, for "there is something too feeble in his voice to be equal to the strains of oratory." Yates was "not distinguished as an Orator," while his fellow New Yorker Lansing "has a hisitation in his speech, that will prevent his being an Orator of any eminence." Governor Livingston of New Jersey he liked, but "he is no Orator," while of Brearley he recorded that "As an Orator he has little to boast of." And so it went.

Pierce perhaps missed the point. These men were not striving to dazzle their audiences. The speakers did not stand on a platform, only in their places, and sometimes they did not even take the trouble to stand up. They had no flags to wave, no chilling samples to flourish, no tables to pound. They never played to the gallery, for the simple reason that there was no gallery; and this saved a lot of time.

Any remark was rated as a "speech," and in the four months that the convention lasted there were, officially, 1,840 of these. Gouverneur Morris, though he was to be absent on business for much of June, delivered the most, 173. Next were Wilson, 168; Madison, 161; Sherman, 138; Mason, 136; and Gerry, 119. Obviously they could not average very long. They were delivered with the idea of putting over points, not for the purpose of setting off verbal pyrotechnics.

On the first day of June the convention addressed itself to what was certain to be one of its toughest problems—that of the executive department.

The jumping-off place was the seventh part of the Virginia Plan:

"Resolved, That a national executive be instituted; to be chosen by the National Legislature for the term of years, to receive punctually at stated times a fixed compensation for the services rendered, in which no increase or diminution shall be made so as to affect the Magistracy existing at the time of increase or diminution; and to be ineligible a second time; and that besides a general authority to execute the National laws, it ought to enjoy the Executive rights vested in Congress by the Confederation."

It seems as though almost every delegate had opinions on this subject. They'd been thinking about it well in advance. Moreover, they were afraid to face the public with anything even remotely resembling a king.

Wilson, Pinckney, and Rutledge favored a single executive, which horrified many, since it did smack of kingship. Sherman thought that the executive or executives should be appointed by the national legislature, as the original resolution provided, since he or they would be no more than an instrument for carrying out that body's will. Madison intervened to suggest that before they decided how many persons the executive department might contain they should first agree upon what powers that department would be given; but the others were more interested in the number, and they brushed this suggestion aside.

Randolph strongly favored an executive of three men. So did Mason, his fellow Virginian, who, however, would also provide for a Council of Revision to assist this three-headed executive, the members of which council would be taken from the judiciary department, he didn't say how.

It was Mason too who brought up the plan to divide the country into three parts, North, South, and Middle, by North meaning New England. Each of these parts should have a member in the executive branch.

This had been discussed in private conversations, "out of doors," but Mason was the first to urge it from the floor. It got little support.

Then they fell to arguing about how long the executive should serve, this matter having been left open in the Virginia Plan. Wilson was for three years, and he assumed that the executive could be re-elected or re-appointed. Pinckney was for seven, but no re-election. Bedford of Delaware was against seven years, for he said that a poor executive could ruin the country in that time, and that impeachment could only be for misfeasance, not for incapacity.

They finally plumped for seven years, though the vote was a close one: New York, New Jersey, Pennsylvania, Delaware, and Virginia aye; Connecticut, North Carolina, South Carolina, and Georgia nay; Massachusetts split.

By then it was time for dinner.

The first thing Saturday morning—Saturday sessions were the same as weekday sessions—Madison was on his feet to move that they pass over the argument about the executive for the present in order to take up the matter of the second branch of the national legislature. This was voted down, 7 to 3, the three being New York, Pennsylvania, and Maryland.

Wilson came up with something new. He proposed that the executive be named by a group of so-called electors, elected by the people themselves in pre-determined districts that would have no relation to state lines. The opponents of this startling idea contended that the people would not know enough to pick good electors and anyway such a system would be clumsy and expensive. It was voted down, 8 to 2.

A motion that the executive be elected by the national legislature was passed 8 to 2.

The minority in each of those votes was Pennsylvania and Maryland.

Now Benjamin Franklin, who so seldom said anything, spoke up. He was disturbed, he said, about the clause that provided regular pay for the executive. He disapproved of it.

The purpose of that clause was clear. In Colonial times the state governors were paid by the colonies, not by the crown, though the crown had appointed them. These governors for the most part were not wealthy men doing a disagreeable duty, but rather titled climbers who were willing to serve a few years in the wilds of America only because the posts paid so well. The Colonial legislatures, however, held the strings of finance, and they would not pass out gubernatorial pay until they had got what they wanted from the visitor. Madison, who had drawn up the Virginia Plan, did not want such a practice on a national scale.

Dr. Franklin thought that the executive or executives

should not be paid at all, except for their legitimate expenses. He had been giving this matter much thought, and since he was getting old and no longer trusted to his memory, he had written down his reasons. He asked the permission of the convention to read them.

The quavering, small voice could only be heard a few feet away, and Wilson offered to read the paper for him. Dr. Franklin thanked him and handed it over.

"Sir, it is with reluctance that I rise to express a disapprobation of any one article of the plan for which we are so much obliged to the honorable gentleman who laid it before us. From its first reading I have borne a good will to it, and in general wished it success. In this particular of salaries to the Executive branch, I happen to differ. . . .

"Sir, there are two passions which have a powerful influence on the affairs of men. These are ambition and avarice; the love of power, and the love of money. Separately, each of these has great force in prompting men to action; but when united in view of the same object, they have in many minds the most violent effects. Place before the eyes of such men a post of *honor*, that shall be at the same time a place of *profit*, and they will move heaven and earth to obtain it." The large number of such well-paying posts in England caused all sorts of trouble there, he averred. "The struggles for them are the true sources of all those factions, which are perpetually dividing the nation, distracting its councils, hurrying sometimes into fruitless and mischievous wars, and often compelling a submission to dishonorable terms of peace. . . ."

It was a long paper, and it embodied a motion that the clause about salary be stricken out.

Alexander Hamilton promptly seconded this; but it was not put to a vote, only tabled for future consideration.

"It was treated with great respect," James Madison wrote in his journal that night, "but rather for the author of it, than from any apparent conviction of its expediency or practicability."

Dickinson moved "that the executive be made removable

by the National Legislature, on the request of a majority of the Legislatures of the individual States." This was rejected, only Delaware, Dickinson's own state, voting for it.

Rutledge and Charles Pinckney spoke in favor of a single executive. Governor Randolph spoke against this, listing four reasons: (1) it savored of and might even lead to monarchy; (2) unity was not needed, a plurality being sufficient; (3) the necessary confidence in the executive could never be vested in one man; and (4) a single executive almost certainly would be picked from the cities, the more crowded sections of the country, which was unfair to the other sections.

Butler spoke in favor of a single executive.

They were still at it at four o'clock, and they returned to it first thing Monday morning, June 4.

Gerry made a motion that the executive should have "a right to negative any legislative act, which shall not be afterwards passed by   parts of each branch of the National Legislature."

Rufus King, in seconding this, said that judges were not the best for an executive advisory council. A judge should propound the laws as they came to him, free from the bias of having participated in their formation.

Wilson declared that executive and judiciary alike ought to have an absolute negative, but consideration of a motion to this effect was postponed.

Wilson moved, and Hamilton seconded, a motion that the end of the Gerry motion be cut out, beginning with the words "which shall not be . . ."

Gerry saw no need of that.

Franklin was against the negative in any fashion. He said that his experience with the governors of Pennsylvania when that state was still under proprietary rule showed him that it gave rise to bribery, that the governor could extract all sorts of favors from the legislators just by a threat of negativing.

Sherman didn't want any one man to be able to stop the will of the whole.

Madison said that if "a proper proportion of each branch"

could repass a bill over a negative by the executive, why, he thought that this would be all right.

Butler warned again against the possibility that a strong executive would soon become a tyrant. "Why might not a Catiline or a Cromwell arise in this country as well as in others?" he asked.

Bedford was opposed to any kind of check on national legislation, executive or judicial or whatnot.

Mason brought up the king bugaboo again. "We are, Mr. Chairman, going very far in this business. We are not indeed constituting a British government, but a more dangerous monarchy, an elective one."

"The people," he added, "will never consent." And: "Notwithstanding the oppression and injustice experienced among us from democracy, the genius of the people is in favor of it; and the genius of the people must be consulted."

Franklin cited the United Netherlands. There was a case, he said, in which a freed people, wishing to honor the man who had done the most to free them, made the Prince of Orange stadholder, only to see that office turned into an absolute monarchy.

"The executive will always be increasing here, as elsewhere," Franklin said, "till it ends in a monarchy."

The delegates sometimes playfully referred to their meeting place as Unanimity Hall. They were being sarcastic, of course. Yet when the motion that would have given the executive an absolute negative came up on the floor, late in the session of June 4, the vote—against it—actually was unanimous.

Butler moved that the executive have the power to suspend any legislative act for a term of time to be fixed by the convention. Franklin seconded this motion. Gerry, however, protested that the power of suspension might do all the mischief of the negative without checking unjust or unwise legislation.

The vote against this too was unanimous.

The resolution at last agreed upon, that the executive negative could be overruled in the national legislature by means of a two-thirds vote in each house, was passed by a vote of 8 to 2.

The delegates were getting along swimmingly now. The ninth resolution in the Virginia Plan, "that a National Judiciary be established," was passed *nem. con.*

It was moved that there be added to this motion the words "to consist of one supreme tribunal, and of one or more inferior tribunals," and this too was passed without a quarrel.

Then Governor Livingston of New Jersey, who had taken his seat only that morning, moved that the words "one or more" be struck out, and this *too* was passed.

Wilson said that he was opposed to the appointment of judges by the legislative branch: it should be done by the executive.

Rutledge could not see giving so much power to any one person.

Dr. Franklin mildly asked why they did not do it as it was done in Scotland, where when there was a vacancy on the bench the principal lawyers got together and appointed one of their own number to the post, "in order to get rid of him, and share his practice among themselves."

Madison too was opposed to the appointment of judges by the legislature, and when he made a motion that this be ruled out he drew the biggest vote yet—9 ayes, 2 nays. It was the first time—and was to prove almost the last—that more than ten states voted on any one thing. New Hampshire still was preparing to send delegates, though Rhode Island remained adamant.

Chapter 7

The Little States Speak Up

THEY HAD CHANGED the hour of assembly back to eleven o'clock, for they found that when the delegates had time to hold informal little conferences before the gavel called them to their seats, the business of the day was disposed of just that much sooner. All the same, General Mifflin of the Pennsylvania delegation was shocked when on Wednesday morning he found outside of the State House door, nobody being near it, a set of the fifteen resolutions of the Virginia Plan. The delegates several days before had been encouraged to make their own copies of the Plan, the better to study it off the floor; and obviously this one had fallen from somebody's pocket.

There was a seven-foot stone wall around the State House, but this did not prevent passers-by from drifting in. The convention's own doorkeeper was exactly that: he was posted outside of the door of their meeting room, not at the street gate.

Mifflin handed the paper to George Washington, who pocketed it without comment.

Though the matter had already been decided, Pinckney of South Carolina asked that the convention consider again the desirability of electing members of the first branch by state legislatures rather than directly. He had served the proper notice of a motion to reconsider, and the first thing Wednesday he made that motion, which was seconded by Rutledge.

Gerry suggested that the people nominate "certain persons, in certain districts" and the legislatures pick a slate from these.

Wilson was still for direct election, and he saw no danger if the districts were big enough.

Sherman, like young Pinckney, preferred election by legislatures; and he was moved to remark that people in the smaller states were on the whole happier than those in the larger states, though he added that some states could perhaps be *too* small for happiness, as witness Rhode Island and her current woes. He implied that he thought his own state of Connecticut was exactly the right size, though he did not say what all this had to do with the manner of electing members of the lower house.

Mason favored direct election.

Madison said that one branch anyway should be elected that way; and Dickinson agreed.

Read was for a whole new constitution, cutting out the states as entities, for he said that to try to amend the Articles of Confederation "would be like putting new cloth on an old garment."

Pierce was in favor of an election by the people in the case of the first branch, and by the states in the case of the second branch, "by which means the citizens of the States would be represented both *individually* and *collectively*."

General Pinckney, Charles Coteswood Pinckney, favored election by legislatures.

When at last it came to a vote—the debate was a long one, and the day hot—Pinckney's motion was defeated, 8 to 3.

Wilson moved to reconsider the vote that excluded the judiciary from a share in the revision of laws. Madison seconded this. It was defeated 8 to 3.

Now Judge Gorham and General Washington exchanged seats. But Washington had something more to do than rap for attention and declare the meeting adjourned. He stood, tall and stern, by the side of the chairman's desk, a paper in his hand.

When he called "Gentlemen!" there wasn't another sound. George Washington had presence.

It is Major Pierce who tells the story.

" 'I am sorry to find that some one Member of this Body, has been so neglectful of the secrets of the Convention as to drop in the State House a copy of their proceedings, which by accident was picked up and delivered to me this Morning. I must entreat Gentlemen to be more careful, lest our transactions get into the News Papers. . . . I know not whose Paper it is, but there it is' (throwing it down on the table) 'Let him who owns it take it.' At the same time he bowed, picked up his Hat, and quitted the room with a dignity so severe that every Person seemed alarmed; for my part I was extremely so, for putting my hand in my pocket I missed my copy of the same Paper, but advancing up to the Table my fears soon dissipated; I found it to be in the hand writing of another Person. When I went to my lodgings at the Indian Queen, I found my copy in a coat pocket which I had pulled off that Morning."

Nobody ever did claim the paper on the chairman's desk.

Next morning, Thursday, at last they tackled the question

of the upper house, which now occasionally some speaker would call "the senate," though in general it continued to be "the second branch." The first branch was never anything but that.

Dickinson said that members of this second branch or upper house should be chosen by the various legislatures; and Sherman seconded that.

Pinckney said that if the method of allotting seats by population were used in the case of the second house, it would result in a body of at least eighty, which would be cumbersome— that is, if each of the smaller states was to have one member.

Dickinson said that the members of this upper house should be distinguished in rank and property, "bearing as strong a likeness to the British House of Lords as possible." Eighty members would be all right to him, or even twice that many. The more the better, he believed. A large second branch would "balance" the first branch.

Hugh Williamson of North Carolina thought that a smaller number of senators, say twenty-five, would be preferable.

Butler said he wanted to know the ratio of representation before he made up his mind. Nobody strove to enlighten him.

Wilson believed that it would be a mistake to have two different methods of election for the two branches of the national legislature. They should be *based* the same, he insisted, or there would be confusion. He wished the senators to be elected directly by the people; and Gouverneur Morris backed him in this.

Read proposed that the executive appoint members of the second branch out of "a proper number of persons to be nominated by the individual Legislatures." Here was at least a new idea; but nobody seconded it.

They were still debating the motion made by Dickinson: that members of the senate be chosen by the state legislatures; and now Madison took the floor to assert that if that motion be agreed to "we must either depart from the doctrine of proportional representation, or admit into the Senate a very large number of members. The first is inadmissible being evidently unjust. The second is inexpedient. The use of the Senate is to consist in its proceeding with more coolness, with more system, and with more wisdom, than the popular branch. Enlarge their number, and you communicate to them the vices which they are meant to correct."

After this they all spoke again, and at even greater length —Gerry, Dickinson, Wilson, Madison, Sherman, Gerry, in that order—but none of them said anything new.

Young Pinckney did have a fresh idea. He thought that the senators should be appointed or elected for life, and he would take them from three classes of states, rated according to size: the first and largest to have three senators apiece, the second two, the third one. Nothing whatever was done about this.

Dickinson's motion had taken all day, and when at last it came to a vote it was beaten, 10 to 0.

"The Committee rose, and the House Adjourned."

Already it was becoming a custom for those who wished for reconsideration of some clause to announce this fact at the close of a day's session, as called for by the rules under which the convention operated, and then the matter could come up the next day. Charles Pinckney had done this Thursday afternoon just before adjournment. He requested another debate on the clause that would have given the national legislature a negative on any state laws that might be thought contrary to the Articles of Union or that might pertain to treaties with foreign countries.

All day Friday was spent on this subject, without any notable result.

Williamson was against taking any police powers from the states.

Gerry couldn't see any need for such a clause, and so he was against it.

Sherman thought that if there was such a clause at least the type of laws that might be subject to a negative should be set forth in it, in detail.

Wilson was in favor of the proposed clause. He pointed out that it was the tendency of the states to encroach upon the central government, a tendency that should be counteracted. He reminded the delegates of how much union talk there had been when the Continental Congress adopted the Articles of Confederation.

"Virginia is no more, Massachusetts is no more, Pennsylvania is no more, we are now one nation of brethren, and we must bury all local interests . . . This language continued for some time. Then the tables began to turn. No sooner were the State Governments formed than their jealousy and ambition began to display themselves; each endeavored to cut a slice from the common loaf, to add to its own morsel, till at length the Confederation became frittered down to the impotent condition in which it now stands. Review the progress of the Articles of Confederation through Congress, and compare the first and last draught of it. To correct its vices is the business of this convention. One of its vices is the want of an effectual control in the whole over its parts. What danger is there that the whole will unnecessarily sacrifice a part? But reverse the case, and leave the whole at the mercy of the parts, and will not the general interest be continually sacrificed to local interests?"

Dickinson would have it all made clearer. Like Sherman, he called for more definition.

Bedford of Delaware declared that the clause was aimed at the small states, which by means of it would lose what little independence they still had.

Madison asked, well, what would happen to the small states if the union fell apart?

Butler was opposed.

When the vote at last was made, at the end of that trying day, Massachusetts, Pennsylvania, and Virginia, the three biggest states, said aye; Connecticut, New York, New Jersey, Maryland, North Carolina, South Carolina, and Georgia said nay; and Delaware was split.

It was a victory for the small states.

Before adjournment, Gerry and King gave notice that they would the following morning ask for a reconsideration of the mode of appointing the executive.

Luther Martin took his place as a delegate the next morning, Saturday, June 9. A smallish man, belligerent, contentious, a heavy drinker, he was attorney general of Maryland, and it was hoped by the small-staters that he would become their spokesman. But he proved to be *too* pugnacious, always ready to fly off into disapproval. What was worse, once he got to his feet he did not seem to know how to stop talking. He proved to be the convention's biggest bore.

Gerry moved that the national executive be elected by the state executives, the governors, "whose proportion of votes should be the same with that allowed to the States, in the election of the Senate." This was evasive, since the convention thus

WILLIAM PATERSON

far had dodged the question of how members of the second branch should be elected. But it was, in itself, a new idea, an attempt to compromise.

It was not well received. Randolph spoke against it, at length; and the only one to speak for it was Gerry himself, who never was very forceful. It was defeated 9 to 0, with Delaware divided.

Then, unexpectedly, the small states, which had been getting increasingly uneasy, found their leader.

William Paterson of New Jersey was not an imposing figure, being sallow and very short. Until this time he had scarcely spoken, but he had been taking everything in. He was a classical scholar, a lawyer—he had been attorney general of New Jersey—and above all, and despite the mildness of his mien, a fighter. He came from Ireland. Major Pierce found him "one of those kind of Men whose powers break in upon you, and create wonder and astonishment." [9]

Now he moved that the convention go back to its debate about the rule of suffrage in the national legislature, the very thing that had been skipped for fear that the small states would walk out. Paterson implied that dealing with this touchy subject was overdue. He implied as well that the delegates from the small states might, for all they knew, be wasting their time; and if that was the case, if the convention was to give all power to the big states, then they might as well pack up and go home right now. Paterson didn't *say* this—he was suave—but everybody knew what he meant.

Brearley, seconding the motion, admitted that it was not fair that Georgia should have as many votes as the great and powerful Virginia, with sixteen times the population. But what could be done about this? The only thing that could be done was take a map of the United States and cut it up into thirteen, or more, or fewer, exactly equal parts.

(No doubt by prearrangement Brearley picked Georgia as an example of a small state, since it was southern. In fact, Georgia, though very small in population, was large in size, and had every reason to think that in time it might extend itself all the way to the Mississippi, a thought firmly denied to such small states as New Jersey, Delaware, and Maryland.)

Paterson himself took the floor again. "The people of America are sharp-sighted, and not to be deceived," he warned the delegates.

"A Confederacy supposes sovereignty in the members composing it," he went on, "and sovereignty supposes equality. If we are to be considered as a nation, all State distinctions must be abolished, the whole must be thrown into hotchpot, and when an equal division is made, then there may be fairly an equality of representation."

There was no more reason why a big state should have more votes than a small state, he argued, than there was that a rich man would have more votes than a poor man. If members of the second branch were to be elected in accordance with wealth and population, he said, then New Jersey "would be swallowed up." He, at least, would not stand for that. He would rather submit to a despot than to such an arrangement.

Wilson spoke too, and Williamson; but it was Paterson who had caused the real stir, and his "hotchpot" caught the imagination of the delegates. Paterson had the last say of the day, too. When it came time to call for the division he got on his feet again.

It had been a hard week, he reminded them, and much hung upon this vote. Maybe it would be better if they postponed it until Monday morning? This was agreed upon.

George Washington, sighing, seeing that this was going to prove a long session, wrote home for more clothes. He also gave directions for the construction of a millrace at Mount Vernon, and asked his nephew and caretaker, George Augustine Washington, how the buckwheat was coming.

Chapter 8

The Beginning of a War

PHILADELPHIA, with a population of almost 30,000, was easily the largest city in the United States. A marvelous metropolis, a major port, it had paved streets and even a system of garbage collection. It was also the most sophisticated city in the land. Like any national capital, it could afford to ignore the presence of celebrities. Your true Philadelphian wouldn't turn his head for anybody less than God.

When Benjamin Franklin had a sedan chair sent to him from France, the first in this country, it did attract a little attention just at first. By the time of the 1787 convention, however, townspeople were thoroughly accustomed to the sight of that chair, carried as it was by two husky trusties from the state jail.

Even George Washington, the greatest hero of them all, came to be a familiar sight. Customarily, needing the exercise, he walked the short distance from Robert Morris's house to the State House; and he was extremely punctual. Tall, straight, serious, a ramrod, he would be dressed, as a rule, in blue and buff, his favorite colors, his regimentals, and would be carrying a long cane, or if there was rain—and there was a great deal of rain that summer in Philadelphia—the umbrella for which he had sent back to Mount Vernon the second week in June.

Neither did the natives crowd into the Indian Queen for a peek at lesser lions. The Indian Queen was a congeries, not a single building, and so thoroughly had the convention delegates made it their own that one dining room was put aside for their

65

exclusive use, so that they could talk freely among themselves without worry about information seeping to the outside world.

They had a great deal to talk about, for they had a great deal in common, being all of the same general class, men of property, men of business affairs, or legal lights. This was no more than natural. Who else could have afforded it? There were no representatives of day workers among them because there were no representatives of day workers in the country. The farmers too were not represented, though there were six southern planters, including George Washington, who had been obliged (he had collateral, of course) to borrow five hundred dollars to make the trip.

Sixty-five men in all, in every state excepting the smallest, had been elected to attend this convention. Three of them declined. Seven others just didn't take the trouble to go. Still others came and went, drifting in and out. Never were all of the remaining fifty-five there at the same time: the average attendance would have been about thirty, so that the sessions, though conducted with great solemnity, were more like committee meetings than conventions.

Thomas Jefferson was to call this "an assembly of demi-gods," and while he might have been sardonic he might have meant that too.

Forty of the fifty-five either were in banking circles or owned government securities, and understandably they sought to protect their investments.

Fifteen owned slaves.

There were three physicians.

The average age was forty-four. There were four who were under thirty, and the youngest was Jonathan Dayton of New Jersey, who at twenty-seven was one-third the age of the oldest, Franklin.

Eight of them were signers of the Declaration of Independence, forty-two were or had been Congressmen, seven were or had been governors of their respective states, twenty-one were veterans of the Revolution.

Twenty-nine were lawyers.

The most amazing statistic of all was that more than half of these men, twenty-nine of them, were college graduates. It would have been hard to find anywhere in the world at that time as well-educated a group of men. Princeton led, with ten graduates.

Some of the standard, accepted class antagonisms were absent. There was no have versus have-nots feeling, for example, there being no have-nots at the convention. The farmer's suspicion of the city man was not on display in Philadelphia, the country being more than nine-tenths rural anyway, and the cities so small. Industry and labor were not locked in deadly embrace here, for there was virtually no industry in America, where labor was not organized. The feeling of those who resided by the sea as opposed to the back-country people of the mountains, a conflict in many of the individual states—Pennsylvania, Virginia, North Carolina—played no part at Philadelphia, where all of the delegates but a few large planters were, in effect, "sea" people. Except in the matter of slavery, an issue that had not as yet engendered much heat, there was very little snarling between north and south. Nor yet was there a plebian-aristocrat rub; for the only persons present who considered themselves aristocrats, the southern planters, were among the most democratic of all in their ideas.

There were of course personality clashes. And there was at least one clearly defined battle of interests, a battle that waxed more bitter with every session. This was between the big states and the little ones.

The small states were Connecticut, New Jersey, Delaware, and Maryland. Georgia, though it had one of the smallest populations, generally voted with the big states. On the other hand, New York, the fifth largest, usually voted with the small states.

The morning was hot and tempers were short when the convention reassembled on Monday.

Sherman of Connecticut started the proceedings with a suggestion that representation in the first branch be in proportion to the free population but that in the second branch, or Senate, each state should have one vote—and only one.

Rutledge proposed that states be represented in both houses according to the "quotas of contribution"—that is, how much money they paid in to the central government.

Butler thought that this was the only fair method. Money was power, he said bluntly, and the states ought to have power in the national legislative body in exact proportion to their wealth.

Dickinson agreed with this.

Rufus King, though he came from a big state, pointed out that no system of collecting taxes had yet been discussed but that what would probably be decided upon was imposts. In other words, states that imported very little, like Connecticut and New Jersey, would be hopelessly outvoted in the national legislature by their more active commercial neighbors, New York, Massachusetts, Pennsylvania.

King and Wilson then moved that "the right of suffrage in the first branch of the National Legislature ought not to be according to the rule established in the Articles of Confederation, but according to some equitable ratio of representation." This would force the issue, bring it to a head. This was the showdown.

Here Benjamin Franklin spoke up. He had prepared a statement, which he asked Mr. Wilson to read.

It was a plea for coolness of temper, for a pause. "We are sent here to *consult,* not to *contend,* with each other; and declarations of a fixed opinion, and of determined resolution never change it, neither enlighten nor convince us."

He pooh-poohed the fear that with proportional representation the small states would be swamped.

"I do not at present see clearly what advantage the greater States could propose to themselves by swallowing up the smaller, and therefore do not apprehend they would attempt it."

He cited the case of Scotland at the beginning of that century, when the Act of Union was about to go into effect. The northern nation was to be alloted only forty members in the House of Commons, only sixteen in the House of Lords, a small minority indeed, and there were many Scots who believed that this meant that their country would be buried by the English whenever there was a division. Had that happened? No.

"The greater States, sir, are naturally as unwilling to have their property left in the disposition of the smaller, as the smaller are to have theirs in the disposition of the greater. An honorable gentleman had, to avoid this difficulty, hinted a proposition of equalizing the States. It appears to me an equitable one, and I should, for my own part, not be against such a measure, if it might be found practicable."

Before the Revolution each colony operated under a separate charter, and these differed widely, some allowing much more freedom than others. Then it would have been impossible to redistribute the land fairly among the existing colonies. Now it was no longer so. Franklin would be perfectly willing to see a part of his own Pennsylvania given over to New Jersey, another part given over to Delaware.

He then came out with a compromise plan so complicated and so vague that nobody took it seriously, and there were many who saw in it a sign of senility, though more likely it was just the wily old philosopher trying to stave off a fight by means of a diversion. Anyway, it made no difference in the debate.

The King-Wilson motion was passed, 7 to 3.

It is notable that Connecticut voted with the majority. This was because Sherman hoped that such a vote would better his own compromise plan, which had received none of the attention it merited, by showing that Connecticut was willing to give in somewhere. Sherman would bank everything on getting an equal vote in the second branch.

However, even if Connecticut had voted, as usual, with the little states, the King-Wilson motion would have been passed.

After that, and with an amazing absence of argument, it was proposed by Wilson that any plan of proportional representation should be based upon the total free population of a given state plus three-fifths of the "other persons," excepting Indians not paying taxes. This was an obvious effort to enlist the southern states in the proportional representation plan, for if they were to vote with the smaller states at this juncture they could decide the issue. The "other persons" of course were slave, never mentioned by that name.

The three-fifths figure was not new. It had been used in the Articles of Confederation as a way of counting the population of slave states in order to reach a basis of taxation, and had in fact been proposed at that time by James Madison himself, as a compromise.

Only New Jersey and Delaware voted against this motion.

Now the dour, implacable Roger Sherman was on his feet again. He in effect restated his plan of compromise when he made a formal motion that the second branch consist of one member, or senator, from each state. Everything, he said, depended upon this. The smaller states, he warned the convention, would never agree to proportional representation in *both* branches of the national legislature.

Ellsworth of New Jersey seconded the motion, which was put to a vote.

It was defeated, 5 to 6. The ayes were Connecticut, New York, New Jersey, Delaware, and Maryland; the nays, Massachusetts, Pennsylvania, Virginia, North Carolina, South Carolina, and Georgia.

The big states followed up their victory when Wilson and Hamilton moved that the right of suffrage in the second branch ought to be according to the same rule as in the first branch.

This was carried by exactly the same vote, 6 to 5, but in reverse.

Here was a crushing defeat for the small states, which, however, refused to stay crushed. It was no answer to the question. It was only the beginning of a war.

To the surprise of many, each delegation was back in its place the following morning, Tuesday. It had been feared that Delaware at least, and conceivably even Connecticut, would walk out.

The fifteenth resolution of the Virginia Plan, which would have referred any plan agreed upon to the several states for ratification, was passed 6 to 3. The minority were small states,

New Jersey, Connecticut, New York, but the small state–big state issue had nothing to do with this.

The convention then returned to the fourth resolution, part of which had been skipped, and debated the length of terms of members of the first branch.

Sherman, backed by Ellsworth, wanted an election for this branch every year.

Rutledge said that in a year's time the members would not get a chance to know their fellow members and to become really useful. They'd hardly have a chance to *get to* the place of meeting from some of the more remote states, he said. He proposed two-year terms.

An aged, rich, and affable bachelor from Maryland, Daniel of St. Thomas Jenifer, now spoke for the first time from the floor. He suggested a three-year term. Too many elections, he said, would tend to make the public indifferent to them, and also would cause good candidates to be reluctant to run.

Madison approved of this, and seconded it.

Gerry proclaimed that New England never would stand for bienniel elections, much less trienniel, and he went so far as to insist that annual elections were the only defense against tyranny.

It was voted, 7 to 4, to make it every three years.

Madison, with Mason seconding his motion, carried a clause that would provide fixed salaries for members of both branches. There was very little discussion. Franklin disapproved of the adjective "liberal" before the salaries, and would have substituted "moderate." Neither was used.

They then took up the question of the tenure of office of those in the second branch, which, it was generally thought, should be longer than that of those in the first.

Spraight of North Carolina wanted it to be seven years. Sherman thought that that was too long, and proposed five years. Pierce proposed three. Randolph, followed by Madison, favored seven years; and seven years eventually won, 8 to 1, New York divided.

Wednesday, June 13, the convention took up the ninth

resolution, which had to do with the judiciary. Governor Randolph introduced it and explained it, and there were no serious objections. Pinckney and Sherman—a curious combination!—proposed that judges should be appointed by both houses of the national legislature, but when Madison urged that the appointments be confined to the second branch as the smaller and more responsible of the two they amiably withdrew their amendment, and it was so voted.

Gerry moved that all money bills originate in the first branch, as being the popular arm, for the people themselves, he said, traditionally held the purse strings.

Butler couldn't see any sense in that, and neither could Madison or King. Read was for it. Charles Pinckney thought it premature. Sherman was against it. Charles Cotesworth Pinckney said that such a provision existed in the constitution of South Carolina, where, having been the cause of much hard feelings between the two houses, it had come to be evaded and was a dead letter.

The motion was voted down, 3 to 7.

Then the Committee of the Whole rose, George Washington resumed the chairman's seat, and Judge Gorham gave the committee's report, which consisted of nineteen resolutions. The house adjourned.

Next morning, Thursday, June 14, Paterson of New Jersey was early on his feet. It was known that he and a few other small state delegates were concocting a counterplan to the Virginia Plan, and it was supposed that he was about to uncork this now. But he wasn't ready yet. He and the other members of his delegation, he said, wished for more time to study the report of the Committee of the Whole. He asked for a twenty-four-hour adjournment. This was agreed to.

The taprooms of Philadelphia must have buzzed with speculation that night.

Chapter 9

Plans, Plans

THE VERY FIRST SENTENCE of what already was being called the New Jersey Plan announced a vital difference between this and the Virginia Plan:

"Resolved, That the articles of Confederation ought to be so revised, corrected and enlarged, as to render the federal Constitution adequate to the exigencies of Government, and the preservation of the Union."

This was outspoken. The Confederation should be changed, strengthened, but not superseded. The Continental Congress should be given more power, not done away with.

There were eight other resolutions.

Number 2 gave much wider authority to Congress, permitting it to levy taxes and imposts, issue postage stamps, and regulate trade and commerce not only with foreign countries but as well among the states.

Number 3 authorized Congress to make requisitions of the various states "in proportion to the whole number of white and other free citizens and inhabitants of every age, sex, and condition, including those bound to servitude for a term of years, and three fifths of all other persons not comprehended in the foregoing description, except Indians not paying taxes." It also gave the Congress power to pass and enforce laws for collecting these, something that the Articles had neglected to do, "provided that none of the powers hereby vested in the United States in Congress shall be exercised without the consent of at least   States; and in that proportion, if the number of

73

confederated States should hereafter be increased or diminished."

Number 4 resolved to authorize Congress "to elect a federal Executive to consist of   persons, to continue in office for the term of   years; to receive punctually, at stated times, a fixed compensation for their services, in which no increase nor diminution shall be made so as to affect the persons composing the Executive at the time of such increase or diminution, to be paid out of the Federal treasury; to be incapable of holding any other office or appointment during their time of service, and for   years thereafter: to be ineligible a second time, and removeable by Congress on application by a majority of the Executives of the several States; that the Executive, besides their general authority to execute the Federal acts ought to appoint all Federal officers not otherwise provided for, and to direct all military operations; provided, that none of the persons composing the Federal Executive shall, on any occasion, take command of any troops, so as personally to conduct any military enterprise as General, or in any other capacity."

Number 5 called for the establishment of "a federal Judiciary," the judges of which would hold office during good behavior, and it stipulated the cases to be heard.

Number 6 decreed that all acts of Congress and all treaties made and ratified by the United States should be the supreme law of the respective states, and that the judiciary of the several states should "be bound thereby in their decision, any thing in the respective laws of the Individual States to the contrary notwithstanding," and authorized the executive to enforce these laws and treaties.

"7. Resolved, That provision be made for the admission of new States into the Union.

"8. Resolved, That the rule for naturalization ought to be the same in every State.

"9. Resolved, That a citizen of one State committing an offense in another State of the Union shall be deemed guilty of the same offence as if it had been committed by a citizen of the State in which the offence was committed."

At the suggestion of Paterson the Committee of the Whole was reconstituted and this new plan was submitted to it for consideration and report. At the same time the Virginia Plan as already altered and amended by that committee was resubmitted to it.

Then everybody who was interested—and practically all of them were—made a copy of the New Jersey Plan for study that night; and the meeting was adjourned.

Next morning a genial, handsome officeholder from New York, John Lansing, who until this time had said next to nothing, opened the meeting with a defense of the New Jersey Plan.

He had the first paragraphs of both plans read aloud by the clerk. *There*, he announced, was all the difference.

He was against the Virginia Plan, he said, for two reasons. It was unauthorized, and therefore illegal; and if submitted to the people it would not be ratified anyway.

Paterson took the floor for a follow-up.

"Our object is not such a government as may be best in itself, but such a one as our constituents have authorized us to prepare, and as they will approve."

Like Lansing, he believed that the Virginia Plan would have no chance of ratification.

He read aloud the Fifth Article of Confederation, which gave each state one vote, and then the Thirteenth Article, which decreed that only by a unanimous vote could the Articles be amended. Had the delegates forgotten these?

"What is unanimously done must be unanimously undone. It was observed that the larger States gave up the point, not because it was right, but because the circumstances of the moment urged the concession. Be it so. Are they for that reason at liberty to take it back? This doctrine may be convenient, but it is a doctrine that will sacrifice the lesser States. The larger States acceded readily to the Confederacy. It was the small ones that came in reluctantly and slowly. New Jersey and Maryland were the two last."

The only expedient that would cure the difficulty, he said

again, "is that of throwing the States into hotchpot."

In addition to being illegal, the Virginia Plan would be "enormously expensive." If Georgia and Delaware were to be allowed two members each in the first branch, that would mean a total of 180 members in that branch. Add to that half as many more for the second branch, and you had 270 men traipsing back and forth across the country at least once a year.

"By enlarging the powers of Congress, the greatest part of this expense will be saved, and all purposes will be answered. At least a trial ought to be made."

James Wilson did not agree. He had been studying the New Jersey Plan, and in his thorough way he had selected thirteen points of difference between it and the Virginia Plan, each, in his eyes, to the advantage of the Virginia Plan. The list, while not wholly fair, is enlightening.

1. The Virginia provided two houses; the New Jersey only one.

2. The Virginia was based on the people; the New Jersey was based on the states.

3. The one had proportional representation, the other equality of suffrage.

4. The one provided a single executive, the other left room for two or three or more such executives.

5. By the Virginia Plan a majority was sure to prevail, but by the New Jersey Plan a minority might do so.

6. The national legislature provided by the Virginia Plan was authorized to make all sorts of laws, but the New Jersey Plan gave added powers to Congress "in a few cases only."

7. The one authorized a negative, the other substituted coercion for this.

8. One provided for impeachment and conviction of an executive, the other for removal by a majority of the state governors.

9. One provided for revision of the laws, the other didn't.

10. The Virginia Plan provided for inferior national tribunals, the New Jersey Plan only for a supreme court.

11. The Virginia Plan allowed for extension of the na-

tional jurisdiction, the New Jersey Plan did not.

12. One extended the jurisdiction "to all cases affecting the national peace and harmony," in the other "a few cases only are marked out."

13. The Virginia Plan would be ratified by all the people, the New Jersey Plan only by the state legislatures.

It was a long speech and a strong one, and like Paterson's speech that had preceded it, it clearly had an effect upon the audience; yet when Pinckney the younger followed it with the sneering remark that if New Jersey were given an equal vote she would dismiss her scruples and concur in the national system, he was only saying what everyone knew.

Ellsworth jolted the session by moving that "the legislative powers of the United States should remain in Congress." This must have been a spur-of-the-moment idea of his. It could not have been prearranged, for nobody seconded it; and so it died.

Edmund Randolph was eloquent in defense of the plan he had sponsored. It was no time to quibble about authority, he said.

"When the salvation of the Republic is at stake it would be treason to our trust not to propose what we find necessary."

He stressed the need of time, the emergency. There might not be another chance, he warned, and if this session failed "the people will yield to dispair."

That was Saturday; and little did the delegates know, as they wended their way to their various inns, that the following Monday morning yet another plan would be dumped into their laps.

John Dickinson of Delaware, a tall, gaunt, gray, ghostlike gentleman, was first up. He moved that the first paragraph of the New Jersey Plan be changed from "adequate to the exigencies of Government, and to the preservation of the Union" to "adequate to the the exigencies, the preservation, and the prosperity of the Union." Debate on this momentous alteration, however, he would like to have postponed, and this postponement was voted, 10 to 0, Pennsylvania being divided.

Plainly Dickinson had been clearing the deck for some-

THE PATRIOTIC AMERICAN FARMER.
J-N D-K-NS——N Esq. BARRISTER at LAW:
Who with Attic Eloquence and Roman Spirit hath Asserted.
The Liberties of the BRITISH Colonies in America.

JOHN DICKINSON

body, and when Alexander Hamilton rose with a sheaf of papers
in his hands everybody knew who this was. Hamilton had so far
been singularly silent at this convention, for him. He was an
imperious young man, single-minded, a person who could not
tolerate opposition, ill equipped for the give-and-take of a convention; and besides, it was common knowledge that his own
vote was impotent, for his two fellow delegates from New York
were members of the Clinton political machine and had orders

to see that Hamilton didn't get out of hand.

Pale, short, arrogant, with a squeaky voice that Pierce found "highly disagreeable," he talked for five hours.

He did not like either of the proposed plans, he said, and he especially disliked the New Jersey Plan. He had therefore prepared a plan of his own, which he held here, but he did not mean to submit this formally to the attention of the delegates, only giving it as a statement of his own thoughts on the subject.

His purpose was to cause the government of the United States to become as much as possible like the government of Great Britain, which, he told the startled delegates, was the best in the world.

He did not believe that a republic could exist for long in such a large and rambling country, but some kind of republic, he conceded, was called for right now. It was what the people wanted.

He quoted, he disparaged, he cited historical precedents, and after a long, long while he got around to reading his plan, first protesting yet again that he was not ceremoniously sub mitting it.

He would have a national legislature of two bodies, the lower to be called the Assembly, the upper the Senate.

Assemblymen would serve for three years and would be elected directly by the people. Senators, who would serve for life, would be elected by electors elected by the people.

The executive authority would be vested in a Governor, to be elected by electors, or, if they couldn't agree, by "second electors." He would serve for life. This Governor had imperial powers. He could make all treaties with foreign nations, though with "the advice and approbation of the Senate." He had complete pardoning power, excepting in cases of treason, when again he must seek the "approbation" of the Senate. He appointed all state governors, and could remove them at will. He was to be supreme commander of the national military and naval forces, and all such forces, even militia, were forbidden to the states. Most astounding of all, the Governor was to have an absolute negative over all legislation, national *and* state, and there could be no appeal from his decision.

Hamilton explained all of these clauses, and others, at very great length; and when he was finished there was a dead silence in the room.

At last somebody moved that they adjourn. It was late.

Hamilton did not put his copy of his plan on the president's desk, but he did give it to James Madison afterward when Madison wanted it for the record. Nothing was ever heard of it again.

Chapter 10

A Welter of Words

ORATORY REMAINED in short supply, but there was plenty of talking. If the delegates couldn't relieve their feelings with flights of rhetoric they could and did hammer their points home, again and again. In the course of a debate as to how many persons each member of the first branch should represent, one delegate pointed out that a hundred and fifty years from then the country might have grown so much that the body would be overswollen, whereupon Judge Gorham interposed to ask if the delegate seriously supposed that what they were creating there in Philadelphia in that summer of 1787 would last a hundred and fifty years? This brought about a laugh, as it was meant to do. Nevertheless, the laugh might have been caused by false modesty or embarrassment at having secret wishes voiced; for if the men in that meeting room were not building for the centuries they certainly acted as if they thought they were.

Careful men, they proceeded carefully, repeatedly testing each clause proposed to put into this instrument they were putting together, tapping it, shaking it, holding it up to scrutinize it from every angle. Spaight's early resolution, that no decision until the final report need be irrevocable, that everything could be reargued on the giving of proper notice, now was taken full advantage of; so that member after member who had seen some pet project of his go down to defeat, now brought it up again, doggedly hoping that the heat or the spate of words might have changed some opponent's mind, and the speeches that had been made before were repeated, usually at greater length.

Impassive, a sphinx, through it all George Washington sat in the sun-backed chair on the dais, his heart being at Mount Vernon. For all the rain in Philadelphia, they were having a drought in Virginia, and this troubled him. His nephew and caretaker, George Augustine Washington, had been ill, and the uncle warned him not to strain himself and not to stay out in the sun too much, but at the same time he suggested that they might take advantage of the dry spell by widening the Mount Vernon millrace, and he gave elaborate instructions as to how this was to be done and with what tools and materials. In this same letter he said that he was glad to hear that the carrots were doing better—they had feared for these early in the summer— but he was still worried, he said, about that buckwheat.

One of the phrases he heard most often, as he sat there, was "In *my* state . . ." or words to that effect. These were old-time legislative workers, and each knew what was wrong in his own capital and was determined that this wrong should be averted in the national government. Many of their experiences at home must have been unfortunate.

Tuesday, June 19, was taken up in an effort on the part of the Virginia Plan supporters, led by James Madison, to try to shake the supporters of the New Jersey Plan out of their position. They were entirely unsuccessful.

Wednesday, William Blount presented his credentials as a delegate from North Carolina. Like so many others, he had been attending Congress in New York when he was notified of his appointment. Unlike so many others, he had nothing to say in Philadelphia.

The first resolution of the report of the Committee of the

Whole was before the house, and Ellsworth, seconded by Judge Gorham, moved to have it changed from "the national government ought to consist of a . . ." etc., to "the government of the United States ought," etc.

He was leery of that word "national," which occurred no fewer than fourteen times in the original Virginia Plan, a model of brevity; and he was not alone there.

Governor Randolph had no objection, and the motion was passed *nem. con.*

Lansing of New York, who until this time had had little to say, proposed that "Resolved, That the powers of legislation be vested in the United States in Congress" be substituted for the second resolution as reported. There were two objections to the setting up of a whole new governing body, he said: the convention lacked authority for such a move, and the public would never accept it anyway. He talked for a long time about this, as did Mason, Martin, and Wilson after him, and the motion at last was defeated 4 to 6.

Another new face, that of Jonathan Dayton, appeared on Thursday. He was from New Jersey, and had been appointed after his father had declined the honor. A captain in the Revolution, he was only twenty-seven, the youngest member of the convention.

The president of Columbia College, William Samuel Johnson—a large, bland, elderly gentleman from Connecticut, a lawyer, son of an Episcopalian minister—took the floor for the first time; and he was not terse.

Before the house still was the second resolution of the report of the Committee of the Whole, which Dr. Johnson discussed. He did not bring out anything new. He said that as he saw it only the New Jersey Plan was calculated to keep the state governments much as they were, while the Virginia Plan would greatly cut their power. Colonel Hamilton alone, he believed, was in favor of eliminating the states altogether. (This Hamilton denied, saying that he had been misunderstood.)

Johnson made no motion. He was followed by Wilson and Madison, who talked for a long time, bringing out nothing new.

The vote on the second resolution as altered, providing for two legislative houses, was at last taken. There were 7 ayes, 3 nays. Maryland was again divided. Connecticut had switched to the big-state side, but only for that one vote, it being the delegates' idea to back Roger Sherman's offer of a compromise, an offer that called for two houses.

General Pinckney moved that the members of the lower house should "be elected in such a manner as the legislature of each State should direct," instead of directly by the people, as the report stood at that time. Luther Martin seconded this. Hamilton was against it, for he thought too much power should not be given to the states. Madison, as he had said so many times already, believed that the people should elect these representatives directly. Sherman was satisfied with the resolution as it stood. Rutledge thought that election by legislatures would be more "refined" than an election by the people "and would be more likely to correspond with the sense of the whole community," though he did not give his reasons. Wilson and King also spoke.

New Jersey, Connecticut, Delaware, and South Carolina voted for this motion. All the others voted against it, except that Maryland was divided.

Then they went back to the old squabble about the length of a first-branch member's term, which at the moment stood at three years. Randolph thought it should be reduced to two. Dickinson approved of three. Ellsworth, Strong, and Wilson all spoke in favor of a one-year term. Madison thought it should be two. Sherman would have preferred one year but he had no serious objection to two. Mason was for two years, Hamilton for three. The motion to change it to two years was at last put to the vote, and New York, Delaware, and Maryland were alone against it, while New Jersey was divided.

That ended *that* day's work.

Ellsworth of Connecticut next morning suggested that the members of the first branch should be paid by the state legislatures, and this raised a hubbub.

Dr. Williamson was for it. Judge Gorham, Edmund Ran-

BRIGADIER GENERAL CHARLES COTESWORTH PINCKNEY

dolph, and Rufus King were against. Sherman was in favor of it, Wilson against. Madison was for fixing the sum and having this in the body of the constitution they were framing. Hamilton was opposed to this. It was finally decided that the national government should pay these salaries, but the vote was close, 4 to 5.

The words "adequate compensation" were solemnly changed to "fixed stipends," but this involved no argument.

Mason favored a twenty-five-year age limit for members of the first branch, and Wilson was opposed to this. Mason won.

Gorham moved to strike out the clause making members of the first branch ineligible to hold other office while they were serving in that branch and for a year afterward. This resulted in a tie vote, 4 to 4, and so was lost; but the argument went on.

General Pinckney moved to strike out the eligibility of members of the first branch to offices established "by a particular state." Some thought that this went too far, others that it did not go far enough, and the rest of the day was spent talking about it. At last the motion was beaten, 2 to 8.

Not only Alexander Hamilton, but all the others who took part in this debate seemed to have a low opinion of their fellow men in politics. The object of the clause, of course, was to prevent members of the first branch from creating unnecessary and well-paying jobs and then quitting the house to fill them. Delegates by and large appeared to think that this is what many of them would indeed do, unless they were restricted.

No such suspicious spirit was evident when the convention took up its next subject, the second branch.

The United States Senate was born in a welter of words. Everybody had ideas on the subject.

The first thing that they did, and without opposition, was change "national" to "of the United States," as had been done in the case of the resolution creating the first branch.

Then Charles Pinckney took the floor, and he stayed there for a long while. This matter of the second branch or upper house being such a large one, he said, in effect, a wide approach to it was called for, and perhaps he had better go into a full description of the state of the nation to receive it. This he did.

He said that because of the peculiar make-up of the American public any thoughts of making the second branch into a sort of untitled House of Lords—and that there were such thoughts was evident from previous speeches—should be abandoned. It just couldn't be done, he said. He then went into a long dissertation on the British Constitution, tracing it back to the dark pre-Christian forests of Germany, with many classical references along the way.

Young Pinckney strove to establish no point. He warned against nothing, except the tendency to think of the second branch in connection with the House of Lords. He made no motion, advanced no new idea, and surely caused nobody to change his mind. Yet it can be assumed that he felt much better when at last he sat down—as did, no doubt, everybody else.

Gorham said that he thought that "there was some weight to the objection of the small States." He did not propose any remedy.

Read said that the states had been in a sort of partnership and that they ought to adjust their old affairs before they opened a new account. He had the western territories particularly in mind. If the Congress made an equable distribution of them, he grumbled, the small states might be more amenable.

Gorham reminded him that the convention had no authority in the case of the western reserves, but that Congress was working on this even then. Mistakes had been made, he admitted, but he thought that this matter could be arranged to the satisfaction of all. In any event—but this Gorham did not say—it had nothing to do with the business at hand.

Wilson was opposed to the appointment of members of the second branch by the state legislatures.

"The election of the second branch by the Legislatures will introduce and cherish local interests and local prejudices. The General Government is not an assemblage of States, but of individuals, for certain political purposes; it is not meant for the States, but for the individuals composing them; the *individuals,* therefore, not the *States,* ought to be represented in it. A proportion in this representation can be preserved in the second, as well as in the first, branch; and the election can be made by electors chosen by the people for that purpose."

He moved an amendment to that effect. The motion was not seconded.

Ellsworth was for the resolution as it stood.

Johnson was against Wilson's plan for electors.

Madison came forward with a bold suggestion. Why not, he asked, postpone the discussion of this, the fourth resolution of the report of the Committee of the Whole, and move on to consider the eighth? Number 8 was the resolution that treated of the suffrage in the second branch, providing that it be like the suffrage in the first branch, that is, proportional. A discussion of that burning topic at a time like this would amount to a showdown. It would be almost a challenge to the small state delegates to walk out.

Nobody commented on Madison's suggestion.

Williamson said that he wanted to know more about the size of this second branch before he could form any opinions on it. He proposed inserting "who shall bear such proportion to the number of the first branch as one to ——" This was not seconded.

Butler made a formal motion—which Madison hadn't done —that they postpone discussion on the fourth resolution and take up the eighth. Madison swiftly seconded this. It was beaten 5 to 6.

The convention voted in the clause that would cause members of the second branch to be elected by state legislatures, 9 to 2.

The clause setting a thirty-year minimum age was voted in unanimously.

It was agreed to strike out "sufficient to ensure their independence" after the word "term."

Then came a clash over the length of the terms for members of the second branch, though there was a general agreement that they should serve in rotation, so as to make for a more stable body. The suggestions ranged all the way from four years to life. It stood at seven in the resolution, and this by a vote of 7 to 3 was stricken out. Then there was a vote on the motion to insert "six years," and this was lost in a tie, 5 to 5, with Maryland still unable to agree. Then there was a motion to adjourn, which likewise lost in a 5 to 5 division, with Maryland split. There was a vote on the proposition to set the term at five years, and this too was lost in a tie, Maryland still split. Finally they adjourned anyway, it being late.

Next day the debate went on, and on, with man after man speaking his piece.

There was a considerable wrangle about the pay—General Pinckney, seconded by Ben Franklin, wanted there to be no pay at all, and this motion lost by but a single vote—and "a compensation" was substituted for "fixed stipends," the idea being to get rid of the word "fixed" and make the clause more elastic. Ellsworth's motion that members of the second branch be paid by their respective states raised a great cloud of talk, and was defeated by only one vote.

When at last that long hot session ended tempers were badly frayed. But the worst was yet to come, as they all knew; for tomorrow they were slated to take up the eighth resolution.

Chapter 11

Dark Threats

IMMEDIATELY AFTER the roll call Rutledge of South Carolina moved that discussion of the fifth resolution of the Virginia Plan as reported by the Committee of the Whole he postponed, and that the convention address itself to the seventh and eighth resolutions.

There was no objection, and it was so ordered.

These resolutions were:

"7. Resolved, That the right of suffrage in the first branch of the national Legislature ought not to be according to the rule established by the articles of confederation, but according to some equitable ratio of representation; namely, in proportion to the whole number of white and other free citizens and inhabitants, of every age, sex, and condition, including those bound to servitude for a term of years, and three-fifths of all other persons not comprehended in the foregoing description, except Indians not paying taxes in each State.

"8. Resolved, That the right of suffrage in the second branch of the national Legislature ought to be according to the rule established for the first."

Delegates sat forward in their chairs, but soon they settled back again; for Luther Martin had taken the floor.

The attorney general of Maryland had a name for forensic brilliance. Perhaps this was one of his off days. If he was drunk, as some thought, he surely must have talked himself back into a state of sobriety. He raged. He raved. He shook his fists.

It was difficult to understand what, if anything, he was getting at. But he was "very vehement."

He said that the national government was meant merely to protect the states, not to govern individuals. He said that if too little power were given it some more could be added later, whereas if too much power were given none of that could be taken away. He said that an equal vote for each state was a practice founded on justice and freedom, not merely policy. He said much more.

He quoted Locke, Vattel, Somers, Priestley.

When he had been talking for more than three hours, he confessed that he was too exhausted to continue that afternoon. But he wasn't finished yet, he warned them. He would speak the rest of it tomorrow.

There was not time for anything else that day.

In the morning, sure enough, Luther Martin had the floor. He kept it for a long while. It is certain that his speech, one of the longest of the convention, and easily the most confusing, changed no vote.

Lansing and Dayton moved to strike out the word "not" in the seventh resolution. This of course would have exactly reversed its meaning.

Williamson, Madison, Wilson, and Sherman all had something to say about this. Madison's was a real speech, well planned. Wilson compared the suffrage system of the Articles of Confederation with the rotten borough system in England.

However, a vote on the Lansing-Dayton motion was put off until the next day, at the request of the New York delegation. One reason for this was because Governor Livingston of New Jersey was ill and so not present. Livingston seldom spoke, but he followed the debates intently.

Now Benjamin Franklin rose, and he indicated that he would speak for himself. This he did, in a low, sibilant voice,

BENJAMIN FRANKLIN

leaning in an intimate manner toward George Washington, almost as if the two of them were alone in the room.

"Mr. President, The small progress we have made after four or five weeks close attendance and continual reasonings with each other—our different sentiments on almost every question, several of the last producing as many noes as ayes—is, methinks, a melancholy proof of the imperfection of the human understanding. We indeed seem to feel our own want of political wisdom, since we have been running about in search of it . . .

"In this situation of this Assembly, groping as it were in the dark to find political truth, and scarce able to distinguish it when presented to us, how has it happened, Sir, that we have not hitherto once thought of humbly applying to the Father of lights, to illuminate our understandings? . . .

"I have lived, sir, a long time, and the longer I live, the more convincing proofs I see of this truth—*that God governs in the affairs of men.* And if a sparrow cannot fall to the ground without his notice, is it probable that an empire can rise without his aid?"

Therefore, he moved that they arrange to have each session opened with a prayer. Roger Sherman seconded that motion.

Now there was some embarrassment and uncertainty. Those who knew him best were well aware that you could never be sure when Dr. Franklin was speaking in earnest. He was a renowned prankster. Nor was he known as a deeply religious man. On the other hand, he would do a great deal to keep the peace.

Hamilton and several others halfheartedly raised objections. They had come this far without a preacher, why not go the rest of the way? Quakers did not customarily open their meetings with prayer, and they were in a Quaker town here. Besides the Friends, too, there were sundry other Protestant sects in town, and even a Roman Catholic congregation: if any one pastor was picked, wouldn't the others feel offended? To summon a preacher at this stage of the game would be to make the folks outside know that they were having a hard time. It might give a rise to all sorts of vicious rumors.

However, it was Dr. Williamson who ended the discussion, when he bluntly reminded his fellow delegates that the convention couldn't call in a minister because it had no funds with which to pay him.

The meeting was then adjourned.

No action ever was taken on the Franklin motion.

Friday there was even more speechifying than usual. Johnson spoke, Gorham spoke, and Ellsworth, and Read, who lulled the delegates with his customary complaint about the way Congress was handling the western reserves, but startled them back into attentiveness by saying that he personally favored the Hamilton Plan, the only delegate who had ever said this from the floor.

Madison spoke at length.

It was Alexander Hamilton himself who struck the sharpest note.

"The truth is, it is a contest for power, not for liberty.

Will the men composing the small states be less free than those composing the larger? The State of Delaware having forty thousand souls will lose *power*, if she has one-tenth only of the votes allowed to Pennsylvania having four hundred thousand; but will the people of Delaware *be less free*, if each citizen had an equal vote with each citizen of Pennsylvania?"

To the consequences of a dissolution of the Union, many of which had been mentioned, he would add another: "Alliances will immediately be formed with different rival and hostile nations of Europe, who will foment disturbances among ourselves, and make us parties to all their own quarrels. Foreign nations having American dominion are, and must be, jealous of us. Their representatives betray the utmost anxiety for our fate, and for the result of this meeting, which must have an essential influence on it. It has been said that respectability in the eyes of foreign nations is not the object at which we aimed, that the proper object of republican government is domestic tranquillity and happiness. This is an ideal distinction. No government can give us tranquillity and happiness at home, which does not possess sufficient stability and strength to make us respected abroad."

Pierce spoke, and Gerry, and Martin, but when the Lansing-Dayton motion at last was put to the vote that vote was what everybody had expected—four small states for, six big states against, Maryland split.

After that a motion was made to accept the suffrage clause in the seventh resolution as the Committee of the Whole had reported it—in other words, to have proportional voting in the upper house—and this was passed by the same vote in reverse, 6 ayes, 4 noes, Maryland still split.

Johnson and Ellsworth, as Connecticut men, were more interested in the eighth resolution, and now they moved that the discussion of the balance of the seventh be postponed and that the eighth be taken up. This was passed, 9 to 2.

Ellsworth promptly moved that this be made to read "that the rule of suffrage in the second branch be the same with that established by the articles of confederation."

If this was not agreed to, he warned the convention, of the states north of Pennsylvania, Massachusetts alone would remain in the union.

There had been mutterings in the past, but nothing as outspoken as this. It gave the delegates something to think about as they filed out for dinner.

Saturday morning the small states tried a new trick, a pathetically obvious one. Brearley of New Jersey, seconded by Paterson, moved that the president of the convention be directed to write to the governor of New Hampshire and ask when those missing delegates might be expected. The assumption was, of course, that when they did come they could join forces with the delegates of the other small states, making things more nearly even.

Rutledge spluttered that he could see "neither the necessity nor the propriety of such a measure."

Rufus King reminded the convention that New Hampshire had been duly notified. He knew from private sources, he said, that the state did plan to send a delegation, which should arrive soon. The delay was due to a personal matter, he said, though he did not explain further.

Wilson said that if such a letter was written news of the fact would be sure to get to the outside world and might well spread alarm.

New Jersey and New York were the only states to vote for this motion. Massachusetts, Connecticut, Virginia, and the Carolinas voted nay. Pennsylvania, Delaware, and Georgia were not fully represented on the floor at just that time, and Maryland of course was split.

There was a great deal of talking then, the first and most eloquent speaker being Wilson, who hammered his favorite point.

"Can we forget that we are forming a Government? Is it for *men,* or for imaginary beings called *States?* Will our honest constituents be satisfied with metaphysical distinctions? Will they, ought they to, be satisfied with being told that the one-third compose the greater number of States? The rule of suffrage ought on every principle to be the same in the second as in the first branch. If the Government be not laid on this foundation it can be neither solid nor lasting . . .

"Bad governments are of two sorts,—first, that which does too little; secondly, that which does too much; that which fails through weakness, and that which destroys through oppression. Under which of these evils do the United States at present groan? Under the weakness and inefficiency of its government. To remedy this weakness we have been sent to this Convention. If the motion should be agreed to, we shall leave the United States fettered precisely as heretofore; with the additional mortification of seeing the good purposes of the fair representation of the people in the first branch, defeated in the second."

Ellsworth and Madison also spoke at length, as did Sherman, and Davie of North Carolina.

Then there rose Dr. Franklin, and his words were soothing —or were meant to be.

"The diversity of opinions turns on two points. If a proportional representation takes place, the small States contend that their liberties will be in danger. If an equality of votes is to be put in its place, the large States say their money will be in danger. When a broad table is to be made, and the edges of planks do not fit, the artist takes a little from both, and makes a good joint. In like manner, here, both sides must part from some of their demands, in order that they may join in some accommodating proposition."

He had prepared such a proposition, and he read it aloud:

"That the Legislatures of the several States shall choose and send an equal number of delegates, namely, ——, who are to compose the second branch of the General Legislature.

"That in all cases or questions wherein the sovereignty of individual States may be affected, or whereby their authority over their own citizens may be diminished, or the authority of the General Government within the several States augmented, each State shall have equal suffrage.

"That in the appointment of all civil officers of the General Government, in the election of whom the second branch may by the constitution have part, each State shall have equal suffrage.

"That in fixing the salaries of such officers, and in all allowances for public services, and generally in all appropriations and dispositions of money to be drawn out of the general Treasury; and in all laws for supplying that Treasury, the Delegates of the several States shall have suffrage in proportion to the sums which their respective States do actually contribute to the Treasury."

It was at least a try, but it wasn't received as such. Both sides pounced upon it. King, Dayton, Martin, Madison, Bedford, Ellsworth—all declared that the motion was unacceptable, that it was no real compromise at all.

Large, fat Gunning Bedford of Delaware caused the greatest stir.

"I do not trust you, gentlemen," he shouted at the large-state men. "The large States dare not dissolve the Confederation. If they do, the small ones will find some foreign ally, of more honor and good faith, who will take them by the hand and do them justice."

Many had been thinking this, but none, until today, had put it in that many words. The delegates were shocked. Rufus King in the last speech of the afternoon sternly rebuked Bedford.

"I am grieved that such a thought entered his heart. I am more grieved that such an expression dropped from his lips. The gentleman can only excuse himself on the score of passion. For myself, whatever might be my distress, I would never court relief from a foreign power."

On that grim note they adjourned.

Chapter 12

Bang, Bang, Illustrious Senate!

THE DECISIVE VOTE came first thing Monday morning. The debate on Ellsworth's motion was finished. The clerk began to call the roll of delegations.

Though members had had a whole weekend in which to think things over, no notable change was expected. Each side had settled down to hold, hold, only hold.

Two other considerations, however, made a vast difference. The Maryland and the Georgia delegations had been reduced to two each, and each of those states had authorized a single delegate to cast its vote if need be.

Georgia ordinarily was a staunch big-state state, but one of its delegates, Major Pierce, had just gone to New York, partly on business, partly to attend Congress, and also to fight a duel; and this morning one of the two remaining Georgia members had misgivings. Houston voted against the Ellsworth motion, but his fellow delegate, Baldwin, a Connecticut man in the first place, new to the South, voted for it. Hence the Georgia ballot was invalid.

As for Maryland, the split was broken for an hour. Daniel of St. Thomas Jenifer, having overslept, was not there, so that the pugnacious Luther Martin was free to vote as he pleased; and he voted *for* the Ellsworth motion.

The ayes were New York, New Jersey, Delaware, Connecticut, and Maryland; and the noes were Massachusetts, Pennsylvania, Virginia, and the two Carolinas.

The vote, then, was a tie, 5 to 5, and the motion, by the

rules of the convention, was defeated. But it had been a prodigiously close thing, scaring the big-staters, who were obliged to remember, too, that those men from New Hampshire might appear any day.

The tie had no sooner been proclaimed when a breathless Daniel of St. Thomas Jenifer entered. Rufus King at once asked that another vote be made; but this was so clearly against the rules that it was not even discussed.

Now there was a pause, for all members realized the seriousness of the situation.

At such times Charles Pinckney usually had something to say, and he was soon on his feet. He viewed several things with alarm, and he reminded the delegates that he himself had framed a plan, a plan—though he did not say this—that was never officially considered by the convention because it was so similar to the Virginia Plan, which had got there first. Pinckney also reminded them that he had once suggested that the States be placed in three classes according to population, the first class to get three second branch members each, the second class to get two, the third class one. Couldn't something be worked out along those lines?

Brigadier General Charles Cotesworth Pinckney did not think much of his young cousin's suggestion. Personally he preferred the plan submitted futilely by Dr. Franklin a few days ago. Nevertheless, *something* had to be done. He proposed that a committee be appointed, to consist of one member from each state, and this committee could examine all possible avenues of compromise and report back to the convention as soon as possible.

This proposal caused a great deal of discussion.

Luther Martin said that he was not opposed to such a committee, but if they thought that they were going to get the small-state delegates to back down they were mistaken.

Roger Sherman favored the committee notion. The convention now was at "a full stop," he said, and it was unthinkable that they should simply quit and go home.

Gouverneur Morris, back from New York just one or two

days before, and in his usual high spirits, went on at some length about the second branch as he thought it ought to be. It should consist of sane and sober men, cautious men, and above all *rich* men, a small body of them, who would check the impetuosity he seemingly took for granted of the members of the first branch. They should be appointed for life, and by the president, who would have no territorial restrictions. Then the ratio wouldn't make any difference. They should not be paid anything.

"The rich will strive to establish their dominion, and enslave the rest. They always have. They always will. The proper security against them is to form them into a separate interest. The two forces would then control each other. Let the rich mix with the poor, and in a commercial country they will establish an oligarchy. Take away commerce, and the democracy will triumph. Thus it has been all the world over. So it will be among us. Reason tells us we are but men, and we are not to expect any particular interference of Heaven in our favor."

It was a brilliant speech, but he did not help. Morris was out of touch. He had no notion of how his fellow members had been working.

Randolph was in favor of the committee, though he didn't hope for much from it. He took the occasion to reprove Gunning Bedford for last Saturday's outburst. He could not see Gouverneur Morris's plan for two offsetting legislative bodies. They would be wrangling all the time, and getting nothing done, he said.

Caleb Strong was for the committee.

So was Dr. Williamson.

Wilson was against it. His chief objection was that it would be formed on the one-state-one-vote principle, the very thing they were trying to do away with; but he added that experience with such committees in Congress had been unfortunate.

Lansing favored it, but he was not enthusiastic.

Nobody was enthusiastic.

Madison was emphatically against it. Like Wilson, he cited the one-member-from-each-state committees of Congress. Anything such a committee could do, anyway, he said, could be done just as well on the floor—and save time.

Gerry was in favor. "*Something* must be done, or we shall disappoint not only America but the whole world."

The first vote was on the idea of committing the problem generally, and it was carried 9 to 2, the two being New Jersey and Delaware.

The second vote, which followed immediately after the first, was for committing it to a "member from each state." This was carried 10 to 1, Pennsylvania's being the only nay.

The committee was appointed then and there, by ballot. It consisted of Gerry, Ellsworth, Yates, Paterson, Franklin, Bedford, Martin, Mason, Davie, Rutledge, and Baldwin.

To give it a chance to function and also to enjoy the holiday, the convention adjourned for three days, until Thursday, July 5.

It was the custom on Independence Day to drink thirteen toasts, one for each state of the union, and sometimes men who started early were surging toward their *second* thirteen by noon. Otherwise the Fourth of July, the Glorious Fourth, was much the same as in later and perhaps somewhat more sophisticated generations. If there were fewer fireworks, still plenty of gunpowder was burned.

The eleventh such anniversary was celebrated with special fervor in Philadelphia, as befitted the birthplace of the Declaration of Independence. The Light Artillery, the City Horse, crack municipal outfits, and the swank Light Infantry, together with an ordinary militia outfit, paraded on the common. The infantrymen fired a *feu de joie,* a regulated, studied, rehearsed, up-one-rank-and-down-the-other volley with blank cartridges, and the artillery fired three thirteen-gun salutes. All over town —at the City Tavern, the Indian Queen, Eppel's, Geiffe's, the Wigwam, the Fishhouse, Gray's Ferry—men were drinking toasts, and at every place there was sure to be at least one in honor of the Constitutional Convention, in which men put so much hope. Indeed, all over the land this was taking place.

The Society of the Cincinnati honored its president general, George Washington, with a dinner at Eppel's, after which they marched in a body to the principal service of the day, that at the German Lutheran Church in Race Street, which was addressed by James Campbell, a lawyer.

The convention attended this service too, in a body, and Orator Campbell addressed himself primarily to the delegates.

"Illustrious Senate!" he cried. "To you your country looks with anxious expectation. On your decisions she rests, convinced that the men who cut the cords of foreign legislation are competent to frame a system of government which will embrace all interests, call forth our resources, and establish our credit. . . .

"Our constitutions were made upon the spur of the moment, with a bayonet at our breasts, and in the infancy of our knowledge of Government and its principles," so that it was little wonder that they were not entirely "accomodated to the temper of our citizens." However, he was confident that all this would be changed. "How fallen would be the character we have acquired in the establishment of our liberties, if we discover inability to form a suitable Government to preserve them! Is the science of Government so difficult that we have not men among us capable of unfolding its mysteries and binding our States together by mutual interests and obligation?"

The delegates did not answer this.

Chapter 13

The Bickering Is Intensified

WHILE OTHERS DRANK toasts, tapped their feet to music, and interrupted spread-eagle speeches with clapping, the eleven members of the so-called Grand Committee toiled; so that they were ready with a suggested compromise, all written out, the morning of the fifth.

"That the subsequent propositions be recommended to the Convention on condition that both shall be generally adopted.

"1. That in the first branch of the Legislature each of the States now in the Union shall be allowed one member for every forty thousand inhabitants, of the description reported in the seventh Resolution of the Committee of the Whole House: that each State not containing that number shall be allowed one member: that all bills for raising or appropriating money, and for fixing the salaries of the officers of the Government of the United States, shall originate in the first branch of the Legislature, and shall not be altered or amended by the second branch; and that no money shall be drawn from the public Treasury but in pursuance of appropriations to be originated in the first branch.

"2. That in the second branch, each State shall have an equal vote."

No official record of the committee meetings was made, and the meetings themselves were of course secret; but it was known that the discussion often was heated and that the final vote was exceedingly close. It was known too that as the oldest and most distinguished member of the committee, and also as the host member, Benjamin Franklin more or less presided. His hand is evident. Indeed, the report is virtually his compromise plan in slightly different form—that each state have an equal vote in the second branch but that money matters be handled by proportional voting.

Gerry read the report, which was probably already known to the members from talk "out of doors."

Gorham wondered if they couldn't be given explanations "touching the grounds on which the conditions were estimated."

Gerry replied that the committee members were of different opinions and that some of those who voted at last for the report as it stood did so only in order to have something to hand back to the convention, not because they were convinced that a one-state-one-vote scheme was satisfactory. These men did not consider themselves bound by the report, Gerry said.

Wilson said that he thought the committee had exceeded its instructions.

Luther Martin was for taking a vote on the whole report at once.

Wilson said that such a vote would be "a leap in the dark." This thing had to be discussed bit by bit.

Madison took the floor for a long speech. He couldn't view the proviso that all appropriations originate in the first branch as any concession on the part of the small states. The second branch was not allowed to negative such bills, but it could refuse to pass them, and didn't that amount to the same thing? The second branch, by the report, would not be permitted to alter or amend such bills. What of that? Couldn't the second branch simply keep refusing to pass a given money bill until it was presented in exactly the form that the members of that branch wished; and wouldn't that, too, amount to the same thing? He did not believe that the little states would wreck the convention by walking out. No matter what Gunning Bedford had shouted, Mr. Madison did not believe that Delaware or any other state "would pursue the rash policy of courting foreign support" or that, if any did, "any foreign nation would be so rash as to hearken to the overture."

Butler said that this expressed his opinion precisely.

Gouverneur Morris talked even longer than Madison had, and he too was not disposed to give in to the small states.

"Let us suppose that the larger States shall agree, and that the smaller refuse; and let us trace the consequences. The opponents of the system in the smaller States will no doubt make a party, and a noise for a time, but the ties of interest, of kindred, and of common habits, which connect them with other States, will be too strong to be easily broken . . . This country must be united. If persuasion does not unite it, the sword will."

Bedford sprang to his feet to say that he had been misunderstood the other day when, he admitted, he had spoken with unwonted warmth; but at least he hadn't mentioned any sword.

He thought that even a defective constitution would be better than none at all. It could be improved later, perhaps.

Oliver Ellsworth explained that illness had kept him from the meetings of the Grand Committee—his place had been taken by Roger Sherman—but he thought that they had wrought well. He was in favor of the report.

Dr. Williamson didn't like the report but still less did he like talk about drawing the sword. He was willing at least to hear the report discussed.

Paterson too was angry because of the Gouverneur Morris speech. He thought that both Morris and Madison were being too rough with the small states.

Gerry, who had presented it, didn't like the report, and he too referred to the sword, but in a different connection: "If we do not come to some agreement among ourselves, some foreign sword will probably do the work for us."

Mason was even more vehement.

"It could not be more inconvenient to any gentleman to remain absent from his private affairs than it is for me, but I would bury my bones in this city rather than expose my country to the consequences of a dissolution of the Convention without any thing being done."

The first proposition of the report, fixing the first branch at one member for every forty thousand inhabitants, was taken up, and the first speaker, Gouverneur Morris, said that property ought to be taken into account as well as the number of inhabitants. This had all been gone over in previous sessions, but Morris treated it as though he had only just thought it up.

Rutledge warmly agreed, and he moved that discussion of the first clause of the report be postponed in order to take up the following: "that the suffrages of the several States be regulated and proportioned according to the sums to be paid towards the general revenue by the inhabitants of each State respectively; that an apportionment of suffrages, according to the ratio aforesaid, shall be made and regulated at the end of   years from the first meeting of the Legislature of the United States, and at the end of every   years; but that for the present, and until the period above mentioned, the suffrages shall be for New Hampshire   , for Massachusetts etc.''

The vote on this ended the day, with nothing done. The vote was 9 to 1 against the motion, Georgia not being on the floor at the time.

Next morning the wrangle was resumed, with Morris, Wilson, Gorham, Gerry, King, Butler, Pinckney, and Davie speaking, some of them twice. No new ground was covered, and nothing was decided except that the "forty thousand" clause should be turned over to a committee consisting of Gouverneur Morris, Gorham, Randolph, King, and Rutledge. These were all big-state men, but the small-state delegates did not object.

It was apparent that nobody had in any way changed his mind. When they returned to the appropriation bills clause it was the same thing all over again, but at least they did get the vote in that day. The clause was passed 5 to 3, Massachusetts, New York, and Georgia being divided.

It was possible for New York to be divided now, for Alexander Hamilton, baffled, had gone back to New York on business a few days before, and Yates and Lansing did not always agree with one another.

In the morning, without any fuss or flare, the telling one-state-one-vote clause came up for consideration.

"This is the critical question," said Gerry.

Gerry himself didn't like it, but he would vote for it rather than get nothing. Sherman spoke for it, Wilson against it. Then they called the roll.

Ayes were Connecticut, New York, New Jersey, Delaware, Maryland, and North Carolina. Noes were Pennsylvania, Virginia, and South Carolina. Massachusetts and Georgia were split.

It was a clear victory for the small states, but it was not final. There could always be a change of alignment when it came time to vote on acceptance of the report as a whole.

There were a few more speeches, and then the convention, before adjourning, voted 6 to 5 to postpone any further discussion of the report of the Grand Committee until the report of the just-appointed committee of five should have been received. It was a troubled weekend, what with the heat and the need to keep an impassive face before the outside world.

"It will be very difficult to frame such a system of Union and Government for America as shall suit all opinions and reconcile clashing interests," wrote Francis Hopkinson in Philadelphia to Thomas Jefferson in Paris, that Sunday. "Their deliberations are kept inviolably secret, so that they sit without censure or remark; but no sooner will the chicken be hatched but everyone will be plucking a feather."

Daniel Carroll, Monday morning, presented his credentials as a delegate from Maryland. This would end the vexatious split, with Jenifer and Martin taking opposite sides on every division, and presumably it would strengthen the small-states bloc. On the other hand, that very same day Yates and Lansing, the two remaining members of the New York delegation, started to close their affairs and gave notice that they were going home. New York had consistently voted with the small states. Nor was there much chance that the Clinton machine would permit appointment of substitutes. The wonder was that it had authorized any delegates in the first place.

The committee of five brought in a two-paragraph report, of which the first paragraph recommended a lower house to consist of fifty-six members, distributed as follows: New Hampshire 2, Massachusetts 7, Rhode Island 1, Connecticut 4, New York 5, New Jersey 3, Pennsylvania 8, Delaware 1, Maryland 4, Virginia 9, North Carolina 5, South Carolina 5, Georgia 2.

The second paragraph read: "But as the present situation of the States may probably alter, as well in point of wealth as in the number of their inhabitants, that the Legislature be authorized from time to time to augment the number of Representatives. And in case any of the States shall hereafter be divided, or any two or more States united, or any new States created within the limits of the United States, the Legislature shall possess authority to regulate the number of Representatives in any of the foregoing cases, upon the principles of their wealth and number of inhabitants."

The first paragraph provoked many angry remarks, until Morris and Rutledge moved to have discussion of it postponed pending a vote on the second. This was done, and the second paragraph was adopted 9 to 2.

Sherman moved to have the first paragraph referred to another grand committee, and Gouverneur Morris seconded this, saying that it was the only case in which such committees were useful.

There was a good deal of talk about the western lands, about slavery, and about the possibility of including the wealth of separate states as a basis for apportioning members of the first branch; and just before the convention adjourned for the day a new grand committee was appointed.

This committee next morning came up with a recommendation that the first branch consist of sixty-five members rather than the fifty-six the smaller committee had suggested. These were to be divided: New Hampshire 3, Massachusetts 8, Rhode Island 1, Connecticut 5, New York 6, New Jersey 4, Pennsylvania 8, Delaware 1, Maryland 6, Virginia 10, North Carolina 5, South Carolina 5, Georgia 3.

"The report is little more than a guess," admitted Gouverneur Morris, one of the committee members.

Guess or no, it raised a furore. The southern states thought that they were being discriminated against. The northern states thought that *they* were. They squabbled all day, and eventually the first paragraph was accepted 9 to 2, settling nothing.

Because before and after each session he had been sitting for the artist Charles Willson Peale, George Washington wore on the dais these days his blue and buff general's uniform, complete with epaulets; but if his face was serene, as always, his heart was heavy.

"You will find but little ground on which the hope of a good establishment can be formed," he wrote that night to Alexander Hamilton. "In a word, I *almost* despair of seeing a favourable issue to the proceedings of our Convention, and do therefore repent having had any agency in the business.

"The men who oppose a strong and energetic government are, in my opinion, narrow minded politicians, or are under the influence of local views . . . I am sorry you went away. I wish you were back."

Though some did not believe this, Hamilton had a heart. When he got that letter he started to pack.

Chapter 14

The Great Compromise

THINGS WERE to get worse before they could possibly get better. It was the low point of the convention. For four days the delegates snarled at one another over matters that were not of immediate importance—the future of the western territories, control of the slave trade, the admittance of new states to the union, and most of all the taking of a census by means of which election to the first branch would be determined—without coming to any real decision.

The North-versus-South feeling was more evident than ever before. Each side was suspicious of the other, and each feared the West. They could fit themselves into the setup as it presently was, but what about the future? If new states came in, on the other side of the Alleghenies, they might be populous but they would surely be poor, and could they not in time take all control away from the Atlantic seaboard states? The delegates assembled in Philadelphia spent a great deal of time proposing and discussing and turning down radical plans for keeping the West under control. Meanwhile, work on the constitution lagged.

The South, frankly, feared that if the northern states increased in population and took over control of the national legislature, they might call for the suppression of slavery, "which," as Butler put it, "some gentlemen within or without doors have a very good mind to do."

Nor was the battle between the small states and the big states forgotten. The small states would not give an inch, and there was a great deal of ominous talk about separating, walking out. The big states might make a league among themselves and the small states could be forced by circumstances to join it. Or the proponents of the Virginia Plan might offer their separate solutions separately to the people of the nation. Or they could simply break up, dissolve. Here was what they all sincerely feared. The country might fall apart.

Not until near the end of the fourth day did Charles Pinckney come up with a concrete suggestion of how to settle the biggest problem—equal representation in the second branch. He proposed an upper house of thirty-six members, to be divided: New Hampshire 2, Massachusetts 4, Rhode Island 1, Connecticut 3, New York 3, New Jersey 2, Pennsylvania 4, Delaware 1, Maryland 3, Virginia 5, North Carolina 3, South Carolina 3, Georgia 2.

After very little fault-finding—perhaps because there wasn't time before dinner—the convention voted this down, 6 to 4.

Monday started on a note hardly more promising, though at least more definite. A vote was taken on the question of agreeing to the report of the Committee of the Whole, as amended, and including the equality of votes in the second branch. This passed, though just barely. Connecticut, New Jersey, Delaware, Maryland, and North Carolina voted for it, Pennsylvania, Virginia, South Carolina, and Georgia against it. New York was gone, and Massachusetts split, Gerry and Strong being for the report, King and Gorham against it.

The small states, having won over North Carolina (though one member of that delegation, Spaight, was opposed), could be said to have scored a victory; but it was a dubious victory, and might be reversed at any time. Still they would not budge. It was equality in the second branch or it was nothing at all.

A start was made toward discussion of the sixth resolution of the Committee of the Whole report, which had been postponed.

"That the National Legislature ought to possess the legislative rights vested in Congress by the Confederation," was agreed to, *nem. con.* Nobody even asked by what right they thought to take away all the power, the very existence, of the Second Continental Congress.

The next clause, "And moreover to legislate in all cases to which the separate States are incompetent; and in which the harmony of the United States may be interrupted by the exercise of individual legislation," had rather rougher sailing. Butler called for some explanation of the extent of this power. He objected in particular to the word "incompetent." What did that mean?

Gorham said that the terms were purposely vague. "We are now establishing general principles, to be extended hereafter into details, which will be precise and explicit."

Rutledge didn't agree, and he backed Butler by moving that the clause be turned over to a committee for further study. This motion met an evenly divided house, 5 ayes, 5 noes, and so it was lost.

Now Edmund Randolph, Governor of Virginia, rose to his feet. He shook his head. He was a troubled and sadly disillusioned man. He had not believed until this morning that the convention would vote for equal representation in the second branch. All the powers given in the report from the Committee of the Whole, he said, had been founded on the supposition that a proportional representation was to prevail in both branches of the national legislature. He had come to the state house today, he said, with several compromises in mind—plans, he intimated, designed to mollify the small states. But plainly those states were not prepared to back down. And with the voting as close as it now had become, where was the use in going on? He proposed an adjournment, to give the big states time to talk over their next move; and perhaps the small states would like to do the same?

Paterson replied promptly. He thought it was "high time" to adjourn, yes, sir. He suggested that the rule of secrecy be rescinded, and that the delegates go home and consult their constitutents. If Mr. Randolph would care to make a formal motion to adjourn *sine die,* he, Mr. Paterson, would second it "with all my heart."

Alarmed, General Charles Coteworth Pinckney demanded to know if Governor Randolph had meant adjournment *sine die* or simply adjournment for the day. He for one did not mean to go all the way back to South Carolina and then return here to Philadelphia on call. Besides, it was silly to suppose that the separate states would agree separately—and beforehand.

Randolph said that he never had thought of adjournment *sine die,* only until tomorrow. He made that a motion, and Paterson cheerfully seconded it. But when a vote was taken it was a tie, 5 to 5, so the motion was lost. The convention could not even rise.

Jacob Broom the Quaker said that a *sine die* adjournment at this time would mean the end of the convention. He didn't need to tell them that. They knew it.

Gerry said that Massachusetts was opposed to an adjournment at this time—it had so voted—because her delegates saw no new ground of compromise. But inasmuch as it would seem to be the opinion of so many states that a trial should be made, Massachusetts would switch sides.

Rutledge too could see no chance of peace in an adjournment, but he too was desperate and willing to try anything.

So they took another vote, and this time adjournment won, 7 to 2, Georgia being divided.

Next morning, an hour or so before the usual opening time, a group of big-state delegates and a smattering of the others as well, met in that fine, handsome, white-walled, high-windowed room where the Declaration of Independence had been signed. They were grim-faced and low-voiced. There was no organization, no formality, nor was any record kept. There were no speeches; but it was the obvious intent of the meeting, an unspoken and certainly unwritten agreement, that the time had come to give in. They didn't like it, but they acceded. They agreed that they would not struggle for reconsideration of the equality in the second-branch resolution, and the small-state delegates, again informally, were so notified.

It was a political deal; and it saved the country.

This was later to be labeled the Great Compromise, or sometimes—since it was Sherman who had first put it forward —the Connecticut Compromise.

Whatever name it be given, it cleared the air. The small-state delegates no longer muttered about taking a walk, and from being obstructive they became helpful.

There were to be further fights. These men were human; and it was inconceivable that they could agree on everything all of the time. But the spirit of the convention was vastly improved, and business began to go again.

Gouverneur Morris started off the formal session that followed by proposing the very thing that the big states had promised they would not do. He moved that the convention reconsider the resolutions of yesterday. Instantly the small-state delegates were on guard again, at the edges of their seats. They might have saved themselves the trouble. Morris's motion was put forward only for effect, for reassurance. Nobody seconded it, and it died.

The convention then took up the sixth resolution in the Virginia Plan as amended and altered by the Committee of the Whole House. This provided "That the national Legislature ought to be empowered to enjoy the legislative rights vested in Congress by the confederation; and moreover to legislate in all cases to which the separate States are incompetent, or in which the harmony of the United States may be interrupted by the exercise of individual legislation; to negative all laws passed by the several States contravening, in the opinion of the national legislature, the articles of the Union, or any treaties subsisting under the authority of the union."

Gouverneur Morris did not like that "negative" clause, and neither did Roger Sherman or Luther Martin. Madison and

Pinckney, on the other hand, spoke in favor of it. The clause was voted down by 7 to 3.

Luther Martin moved this resolution: "That the Legislative acts of the United States made by virtue and in pursuance of the Articles of Union, and all treaties made and ratified under the authority of the United States, shall be the supreme law of the respective States, as far as those acts or treaties shall relate to the said States, or their citizens and inhabitants; and that the Judiciaries of the several States be bound thereby in their decisions, anything in the respective laws of the individual States to the contrary notwithstanding," a most lawyerly resolution, which was agreed to *nem. con.*

They had postponed discussion of the sixth resolution in order to take up the two most contentious ones, the seventh and eighth, which established the two houses of the national legislature. Now that they had returned to the sixth resolution and had disposed of it, they moved to the ninth.

This would establish the executive.

The first clause provided that the executive should consist of "a Single Person," and here there was no argument, all being in agreement.

It was different when the second clause, "to be chosen by the National Legislature," came up.

Morris was against it. He thought that the executive ought to be elected directly by the people. Otherwise he would become a mere tool of the legislature. He moved that the words "National Legislature" be stricken out of the resolution and "citizens of the United States" substituted.

Sherman was for the resolution as it stood, and so were Wilson and Pinckney and Colonel Mason, who shared the opinion of the others that the public could not be expected to make a good choice, for asking that would be like "offering a trial of colors to a blind man."

The Morris motion was voted down, 9 to 1, only Pennsylvania, his own state, being in favor of it.

Martin of Maryland moved that electors be chosen by the

various state legislatures, and Broom seconded this, but it was lost by an 8-to-2 vote.

At last the clause "to be chosen by the National Legislature" was adopted unanimously.

Action on the clause "for the term of seven years" was postponed.

". . . to carry into execution the national laws" was passed *nem. con.*

". . . to be ineligible a second time" raised a discussion. Houston of New Jersey, the Princeton professor who until this time had had nothing to say from the floor, strongly objected to it. He moved to strike it out, and Sherman seconded the motion. Gouverneur Morris too spoke in favor of this motion. To deny the executive a second term, he said, would be to take away from him the strongest incentive to do a good job. "It would be like saying to him: 'Make hay while the sun shines.'"

The motion was passed, 6 to 4.

Then they got back to the seven-year term. Broom was for making it shorter. Dr. McClurg of Virginia moved to strike out "seven years" and insert "during good behavior," and Morris seconded this. Broom was for it, Sherman against it. Madison was for it. Mason could see no difference between "good behavior" and "life," and he feared the McClurg motion as tending toward monarchy. Then they all spoke again; but they were brief.

The motion was voted down, 6 to 4.

By the same vote it was agreed to refrain from striking out the words "seven years."

Before adjournment it was agreed that the next morning they would reconsider the vote that had stricken out "to be ineligible a second time."

That was Tuesday, a good day. They got a lot done Tuesday.

Chapter 15

A Fruitful Week

THE SUPREME COURT was the next item on the agenda. They cleared the decks by postponing until the following day a motion to reconsider the vote on the clause denying the executive the right to succeed himself, and by passing *nem. con.* the tenth resolution contained in the report of the Committee of the Whole, the one that gave the executive power to negative any law unless it was repassed by a two-thirds vote of each branch.

Then they turned to the eleventh resolution. The first clause, which simply stipulated that there should be *a* supreme court, with no mention of inferior federal courts, was passed *nem. con.* The next, providing that the members of this court be appointed by the second branch of the national legislature, presented more problems.

Judge Gorham said he thought that the justices should be appointed by the executive, with the advice and consent of the upper house, as had been done successfully in Massachusetts for a hundred and forty years. He did not make a motion to this effect, but the next speaker, Wilson, did. Wilson, however, left out the upper house. This was perhaps unwise, for there was a strong current of feeling against giving the executive too much power.

Luther Martin was "strenuous" for the resolution as originally reported by the Committee of the Whole. Sherman too favored this, and Mason of Virginia had a few cautious remarks to make before it went to a vote.

The Wilson motion was defeated, 6 to 2.

Judge Gorham then put his suggestion, the advice-and-consent one, in the form of a motion. This resulted in a 4 to 4 tie, and so was defeated.

Madison moved that the justices be nominated by the executive, which nominations would become appointments "if not disagreed to within   days" by two-thirds of the second branch. Discussion on this was postponed to the next day.

The "good behavior" and "fixed compensation" clause was accepted without question, but the "encrease or diminution" clause was opposed by Morris, who moved to strike out the words "encrease or." This motion was carried, 6 to 2.

The twelfth resolution simply read "That the national Legislature be empowered to appoint inferior Tribunals." This was agreed upon without dissent.

The thirteenth resolution was passed in the same easy manner, though only after it had been somewhat reworded on the motion of James Madison.

The fourteenth pertained to the admittance of new states into the union, and this met with no opposition.

The fifteenth graciously permitted the Continental Congress to continue in being "for the completion of their engagements" until the new government was prepared to take over. The first part of this was voted down, 6 to 3, and the second part died automatically.

In the sixteenth it was resolved "That a republican Constitution, and its existing laws, ought to be guaranteed to each State by the United States."

This stirred talk. Gouverneur Morris thought it highly objectionable. He certainly didn't want to promise that such laws as existed right then in Rhode Island should be guaranteed.

"The object is merely to secure the States against dangerous commotions, insurrections and rebellions," Wilson explained.

Mason and Randolph spoke in favor of it, and that other ardent Virginian, James Madison, moved to substitute for it: "That the constitutional authority of the States shall be guaranteed to them respectively against domestic as well as foreign violence." Dr. McClurg seconded this.

Houston was afraid that the resolution might perpetuate existing state constitutions, some of which were pretty bad—Georgia's, for instance.

Luther Martin was for leaving the states to suppress their own rebellions.

Gorham begged to disagree. Without some such provision in the constitution, he declared, some adventurer might set up a monarchy in one state, "might gather together partizans from all quarters, might extend his views from State to State, and threaten to establish tyranny over the whole, and the General Government be compelled to remain an inactive witness of its own destruction."

Randolph moved to add, as an amendment to Madison's motion, "and that no State be at liberty to form any other than a republican government." Madison seconded this.

Rutledge thought the guarantee was unnecessary. The central government had the authority, if it had the means, to co-operate with any state in subduing a rebellion.

Wilson moved, as perhaps a better expression of the idea, "that a republican form of Government shall be guaranteed to each State; and that each State shall be protected against foreign and domestic violence."

This appeared to please everybody, so Randolph and Madison withdrew their motions, and Wilson's motion was passed unanimously.

Luther Martin it was who, having given notice, moved to reinstate the words "to be ineligible a second time" into the ninth resolution.

Gouverneur Morris thought that the executive ought to serve for two years or else for life, and he was, as before, in favor of a direct popular election. The reason people said that a territorially large republic could not be a success was because the executives of such republics were not strong enough to reach into the four corners of the land. If the executive was denied any hope of re-election he would not be encouraged to do his best, and if he was appointed by the national legislature he could easily become the creature of that body instead of standing for the public as "against the great and the wealthy, who in the course of things will necessarily compose the legislative body." He made the point, as many had made it before this, that the three sections of government—executive, legislative, and judicial—should by all means be kept independent one from the others.

Randolph was for Martin's motion.

King did not like the ineligibility clause. He favored having the executive elected by electors.

Paterson favored the same thing, and he thought that there should be one elector for each of the smallest states, two for each middle-sized state, and three for the largest.

Wilson was for an election by the people, and so was Madison, though Madison would not be opposed to electors.

Gerry was shocked that anyone would even dream of a direct election. "The people are uninformed, and would be misled by a few designing men . . . The popular mode of electing the Chief Magistrate would certainly be the worst of all." He favored electors picked by the state governors.

It was voted unanimously that the convention should "reconsider generally" the ninth resolution.

Ellsworth proposed electors to be chosen by the state legislatures, one for each state of less than 200,000, two for states of between 200,000 and 300,000, and three for each state with a population greater than 300,000.

Rutledge was still in favor of the national legislature naming the executive, and he still thought that the executive should not be permitted to succeed himself.

Gerry proposed twenty-five electors, to be distributed thus: New Hampshire 1, Massachusetts 3, Rhode Island 1, Connecticut 2, New York 2, New Jersey 2, Pennsylvania 3, Delaware 1, Maryland 2, Virginia 3, North Carolina 2, South Carolina 2, Georgia 1.

The question "Shall the National Executive be appointed by electors?" was answered in the affirmative, 6 to 3, with Massachusetts divided.

ELBRIDGE GERRY

The question "Shall the Electors be chosen by the State Legislatures?" was answered in the affirmative, 8 to 2.

Discussion of the ratio of electors state by state was postponed.

Luther Martin then formally moved that the ineligibility clause be reinserted into resolution nine.

This was put in the form of two questions: "Shall the Executive be ineligible a second time?" and "Shall the Executive continue for seven years?"

On the first the vote was no, 8 to 2, the minority being made up of the Carolinas.

On the second the vote was no by 5 to 3.

Ellsworth then moved that the term be fixed at six years, and this was carried 9 to 1, Delaware being the 1.

The method of electing an executive by means of electors chosen by state legislatures having been decided upon, then, it remained to determine how many of these electors there should be. Madison warned the session that one to every 100,000 of population—which he understood was roughly what was planned—should not be an inflexible figure. The smallest state would soon rate three, he said, and the ratio decided upon should be only temporary or else so varied that it would adjust itself to the growing population.

Gerry reproduced his previously read table of twenty-five, now in the form of a motion.

After a few half-hearted attempts to have Georgia and New Hampshire granted two electors each rather than one— New Hampshire had friends on the floor, it seemed, even though she did not have any delegates there—the motion was passed, 6 to 4.

Then came the matter of impeachment. Charles Pinckney and Gouverneur Morris were against it, Davie and Wilson and Mason were for it. Benjamin Franklin pointed out that elsewhere in the world ordinarily the only recourse against tyranny was assassination, an act that not only took a man's life but also deprived him of a chance to clear his name. We certainly didn't want that, now did we? Gouverneur Morris admitted that impeachment might be all right in some cases, but those cases ought to be enumerated and defined.

Madison spoke for the motion, and Gerry, and Randolph; and then a curious thing happened. Gouverneur Morris announced that the arguments for impeachment had caused him to change his mind. The motion was passed, 8 to 2.

The clause arranging for "a fixed compensation" for the executive was agreed to *nem. con.*, and only one state, New Jersey, voted against the clause providing that this be done out of the national treasury.

Gerry and Morris moved that electors must not be members of the national legislature, nor officers of the United States, nor yet be themselves "eligible to the supreme magistracy," and this was passed *nem. con.*

The subject was still on the floor next morning, Saturday, July 21, when Dr. Williamson moved that the electors be paid for their services, and this was voted in *nem. con.* but the delegates quickly switched to the question of having the national judges associated with the executive in the revision of laws when this was deemed advisable.

It was Wilson who brought it up. He admitted that it had been thoroughly discussed and voted down at a previous session, but he thought it was important enough to rate a rehash.

"Laws may be unjust, may be unwise, may be dangerous, may be destructive; and yet may not be so unconstitutional as to justify the Judges in refusing to give them effect."

There were not many to agree with him, though Madison seconded his motion, and Ellsworth spoke for it. Gerry said that this would give the judges a double negative, since they could always declare a passed law unconstitutional.

In this debate, as in all of the others that touched upon any aspect of the national legislature, it was remarkable that no delegate ever seemed to think that there would be many non-rascals in that body. North or South, big state or little state, they went on the assumption that not merely a few but a large majority of the legislators would require sharp watching. Low as was their opinion of the common man, the man in the street, their opinion of the average congressman-to-be was lower still.

Martin spoke against Wilson's motion, as did Rutledge and Gorham, and eventually it was defeated, 4 to 3, with Pennsylvania and Georgia divided, and New Jersey not voting.

This took up a large part of Saturday afternoon, but there was still time to pass by a *nem. con.* vote the clause in the tenth resolution giving the executive a qualified negative, and to discuss Madison's postponed motion that the judges of the supreme court be nominated by the executive, which nominations would become appointments in ten days unless two-thirds of the second branch had voted disagreement with them in the meanwhile.

The Madison motion was defeated, 3 to 6; and another motion, approving the resolution as it stood—that is, that the judges be appointed by the second branch—was passed with a reverse vote, 6 to 3.

It had been a fruitful week.

Chapter 16

The Committee of Detail

THE NEW HAMPSHIRITES showed up at last, to present their credentials and apologize for being more than two months late. They were John Langdon and Nicholas Gilman.

Resolution 17, "That provision ought to be made for future amendments to the articles of Union," met no opposition.

Resolution 18, requiring that the legislative, executive, and judicial departments of the states be bound by oath to support the articles of Union, caused a little talk. Williamson thought that it should work the other way as well—that is, that federal officers should be pledged to support the individual states. Wilson was not fond of oaths. "A good government does not need them, and a bad one could not or should not be supported." Gorham saw no harm in them, and Gerry conceded that they just might do some good. The resolution was voted in, *nem. con.*

This was getting to be, in all faith, Unanimity Hall.

Resolution 19 referred the proposed constitution to assemblies to be chosen by the people for the express purpose of ratifying it.

Ellsworth moved that it be ratified by the state legislatures instead of the people in convention, and Paterson seconded this. Mason did not agree. "The Legislatures have no power to ratify it. They are the mere creatures of the State Constitutions, and can not be greater than their creators." Randolph said that the state legislators, fearing a loss of power, would be prejudiced against the new constitution. Gerry thought that whatever happened it certainly shouldn't be left to the people: "*They* will never agree on anything," Gorham repeated Randolph's argument about the fear of losing power, and added that most state legislatures consisted of two houses, which might mean delay, and they were concerned with other matters, routine business, which might mean even more delay. Ellsworth spoke for the legislators. Williamson said why not have both— that is, why not authorize the state legislatures to pick delegates to ratifying conventions?

Gouverneur Morris, who after all came from a centrally located state, moved for one big convention, a national affair, the delegates to be chosen by the people. Nobody seconded this.

When the proposition was put that the plan at last agreed upon should be passed first through Congress and then put up to state conventions, the delegates of which would be chosen by the public, all excepting Delaware voted for it.

The method of electing a national executive gave the convention more trouble than any other question, but close behind it was the matter of the second branch, or upper house. Rufus King proposed that its members vote separately, and not, as was done in the Continental Congress and right here in the convention, by state units. But, how many should there be from each state? Gouverneur Morris was in favor of three instead of two— if, that is, a majority were to be a quorum, as was the usual rule. Otherwise, fourteen men could control the whole body in the absence of the others, and that was too small a group to entrust with such power.

Gorham reminded him that sundry territories were already knocking for admission into the union as states—Kentucky, Vermont, Maine, and Franklin (which became Tennessee).

Mason thought that three from each state would be too many, if only because it would be so expensive. Evidently most of the others thought so too, for when it came to a vote only Pennsylvania, Morris's own state, was for it. A motion for two from each state then was passed, only Maryland being opposed.

Houston and Spaight moved that the whole business of the national executive be reconsidered yet again, and this was ordered for the next day.

General Pinckney rose ominously, and he said that unless there was written into the constitution some guarantee that slavery would not be abolished, and that there would be no taxes on exports, he would consider himself bound by his acceptance oath to refuse to sign the thing.

This had been a long time coming, and everybody took it seriously. The South stood to lose millions and be twisted out of a whole way of life if slavery was abolished, and it feared that the New York and New England shipping industry was planning to arrange for export fees, which might ruin the South's trade in rice and indigo: cotton did not amount to much.

It was agreed to appoint a committee to study this and other questions—the Committee of Detail, it was called, informally, from the beginning. Should there be ten members of this committee, one from each state? Only Delaware favored that. Seven? This was lost on a tie vote, 5 to 5. A motion to make it a committee of five, however, was passed unanimously, and the following day the committee was elected from the floor. The committee consisted of Rutledge, Gorham, Ellsworth, Wilson, and Randolph—two southerners, two New Englanders, and one from a middle state. A motion to discharge the Committee of the Whole from the propositions submitted to the convention as the basis of a constitution, and to refer these to the Committee of Detail, was passed unanimously.

On that same day they tackled once again the complex problem of an executive.

Houston moved that the executive be appointed by the national legislature, otherwise good men wouldn't consent to stand for the office. Gerry disagreed, and said that if this were done it would be necessary to reinsert the no-second-term clause, lest the executive become a pawn of the legislators. Strong didn't agree with *that*. Williamson favored a seven-year term and no re-election. In fact he really favored (though he despaired of getting it) three executives, one for the South, one for the North, one for the middle states. Just a single executive, alone, smelled to him of monarchy.

"It is pretty certain that we will at some time or other have a King," he said, "but I want no precaution omitted that might postpone the event as long as possible."

Houston's motion was carried, 7 to 4.

Then, about the no-re-eligibility clause, there was a question of whether the executive shouldn't have a longer term. In general, those who supported the ban on re-election supported also a long term. Eleven years, thought Martin aloud. Fifteen, muttered Gerry. "Why not make it twenty?" asked a sarcastic Rufus King. "That's the medium life of princes."

Wilson, sensing trouble, moved, unsuccessfully, to postpone the debate.

Gerry proposed that the question be referred to the Committee of Detail.

Until this time they had been tramping back and forth over long-familiar ground, but now Wilson submitted something new. Let the executive be elected for six years by not more than fifteen members of the national legislature who would be chosen by lot. This was, he confessed, not a "digested" idea, and he thought that it might meet some opposition.

He was right. It did. Gerry, for one, thought that it would mean "committing too much to chance," and the vote to postpone further discussion of it was unanimous.

They tried hard, so hard, to find an answer. Every proposal had some grave objection to it, sometimes a whole series of objections.

Ellsworth moved that the executive be appointed by the national legislature unless he was already in office and was seeking a second term, in which case he would be elected by electors. Gerry thought that *any* election by the national legislature would be "radically and incurably wrong." He wanted election by the state governors. Madison summed it all up in a long and able speech, without contributing anything new.

Ellsworth's motion was defeated, 7 to 4.

Pinckney moved that a six-year term be established with the proviso that no man could serve more than six out of every twelve years. This was ingenious. It would keep a good, experienced executive on hand for later use, giving him a chance meanwhile to mix with the people, an action Benjamin Franklin defined as a "promotion" rather than a "degradation," since in a republic the people were the rulers, the officers the servants. Mason thought that this was a good idea, and so did Gerry.

Williamson suggested that each elector vote for three possible candidates of this choice, only one of whom could come from his own state. Here, too, was a new notion.

John Dickinson observed that one of the faults chiefly found in the electoral system was that electors would only vote for—would, in all probability, only *know*—men from their respective states. Well, it was true that a man would be best known and most appreciated in his native state, so why should not each state nominate its own best citizen, or favorite son, and have either the national legislature or a board of electors named by the legislature pick one from this panel?

At long last Pinckney's motion lost.

They were still at it the next morning, Thursday, July 26, when Mason's motion that the term be set again at seven years and the no-re-eligibility clause be reinserted was passed, after much discussion, 6 to 3.

Mason also moved that the Committee of Detail be instructed to receive a clause that would prevent the seat of the national government from being established in a state capital, and Gerry proposed to amend this to read a state capital or any large commercial city. The proposal caused such a stir—Gouverneur Morris, for example, feared that it would raise hard feeling between Philadelphia and New York, the two chief contenders for the honor—that Mason withdrew it.

The Committee of Detail would have plenty of work without it. To these five men were given sets of the resolutions adopted by the convention so far, twenty-two in number, as they stood after the latest changes. To them also were given copies of the Paterson, or New Jersey, plan and Charles Pinckney's own private plan, which latter never had been formally submitted to the convention because it was almost identical with the original Virginia Plan.

Finally, the five men were given ten days in which to study and formulate a report. A great deal would hang on that report.

The convention adjourned until August 6.

Chapter 17

No Rest for the Weary

GEORGE WASHINGTON went fishing. More accurately, he went on a fishing trip with his friend and host Robert Morris, who wished to see if he could coax some trout out of Trout Creek on Jane Moore's property near Valley Forge. They borrowed Gouverneur Morris's phaeton, but hitched the General's own horses to it; and when they got there the General decided that instead of wading in the stream he would revisit the scene of his 1777/78 encampment. He had never seen Valley Forge in the summer.

It is a lovely spot, though Washington would hardly have remembered it as such. He wandered about for some hours, seeing the fallen-in huts, the trenches, the moldering redoubts, collapsed gun platforms. What he thought about it we do not know, for though he recorded the visit in his diary that night, characteristically he wrote nothing about his feelings. Neither did he say whether Robert Morris caught anything. In that same diary at that same sitting, however, he related at length a talk he had enjoyed with some farmers encountered in a field on the way back to the Widow Moore's house. He had asked them about buckwheat, and they had been very helpful, giving him information that he could and would pass along to George Augustine Washington at Mount Vernon. He devoted four

times as much diary space to the buckwheat meeting as he did
to the Valley Forge visit.

It was good to be out of doors again, away from all those
speeches. He tried his own luck at fishing—and caught nothing
—Friday, August 3, on the Delaware. That same day he visited
the Trenton Iron Works, the biggest in the country, capable of
handling fourteen tons of ore at a time. The next day he had
better luck, hooking a few perch. He dined that afternoon
with General Philemon Dickinson at "The Hermitage," on the
New Jersey side. His bleeding, half-frozen soldiers had staggered
past this very house early on the morning of December 26,
1776, on their way to Trenton and a stunning victory over the
Hessians; but Washington did not even mention this in his
diary. He was back in Philadelphia the night of the fifth, so as
to be ready to preside at the Constitutional Convention next
morning.

During the recess the Maryland delegation changed somewhat: Luther Martin had gone to New York on business, and
James McHenry, who had been called away by the serious illness
of his brother, returned. John Francis Mercer, a young man
who had recently married money, appeared and took his place
on the delegation; but he did not stay long, for he was shocked
at the highly centralized government the convention appeared
to be setting up, and he soon went back to his bride.

Pierce Butler was visiting his family in New York. He had
left them there when he quit Congress for the convention,
because he thought that New York was a less unhealthy place
in the summer. All the New Jersey delegates had gone home,
and Sherman and Judge Johnson had gone back to Connecticut.
General Pinckney was visiting some friends in Bethlehem, Pa.

For those who remained in the city, there were diversions.
The drama was in bad repute at the time, but a New York
company of actors was in town putting on plays which it was
careful to bill as "operas" or "concerts," and Philadelphia,
despite the Quakers, must have been almost as gay as it had been
during the '77/'78 occupation. It boasted, among other attrac-
tions, a fine private library, established by Ben Franklin's

Philosophical Society, the facilities of which were thrown open to the delegates. Most of their time, however, must have been spent in catching up on their correspondence.

Again and again they apologized for their lack of the sort of news the folks back home really wanted to hear—news of the convention itself, what went on behind those closed doors. They were scrupulous about this. James Madison, Sr., suggested to James Madison, Jr., that though admittedly he could not tell what the convention was *doing*, still perhaps if he would tell in his letters what it was *not* doing, that would help to give the outside world some inkling; but the son refused to fall in with this scheme.

The delegates in part made up for this secrecy by speculating on the amount of work that still lay ahead of the convention. It was great.

"How long before the business of Convention will be finished is very uncertain, perhaps not before September if then," Alexander Martin wrote to the governor of his state, North Carolina.

"I think the business of the Convention will not be completed until the first of September," the New Hampshire delegate, Nicholas Gilman, wrote to a relative.

"I hope we may succeed," Pierce Butler wrote to his son. "Our country expects much of us. We have sat every day since the 25th of May till last Saturday, when we adjourned for one week."

The five members of the Committee of Detail, to be sure, had no time for picnics and fishing trips and "concerts." They toiled mightily. Now for the first time an actual constitution was being put down on paper.

These were not timid men. They did not think themselves limited to the arrangement, in good order, of the resolutions the convention had passed. They went much further than this. They drew on the New Jersey Plan and perhaps to a smaller extent on the Pinckney Plan, and they consulted sundry state constitutions. It is likely too, from internal evidence, that they studied again the report of August 22, 1781, by the Committee of the Old Congress appointed to prepare the Articles of Confederation. Two of the members of the Committee on Detail, Ellsworth and Randolph, had been members of that older committee.

Randolph made the first draft, and it is probable that James Wilson made a draft of his own. John Rutledge made marginal notes. They all worked on it, going over it again and again.

They had it ready on time, thanks to a night job done at the Dunlap & Claypoole printing plant amid the greatest secrecy. It was a folio pamphlet of seven pages, with wide margins so that the delegates could make notes. Sixty of these were printed, and they were guarded like golden ingots. Monday morning, August 6, they were passed out.

Chapter 18

"We the People—"

"WE THE PEOPLE of the States of New Hampshire, Massachusetts, Rhode-Island and Providence Plantations, Connecticut, New York, New-Jersey, Pennsylvania, Delaware, Maryland, Virginia, North-Carolina, South-Carolina, and Georgia, do ordain, declare, and establish the following Constitution for the Government of Ourselves and our Posterity."

That was how it started, with a sweep, reminding everybody that this was not a mere agreement between states but rather a declaration on the part of a sovereign people. The comparatively namby-pamby Articles of Confederation had started with "Articles of Confederation and perpetual Union between the States of Newhampshire, Massachusetts-bay, Rhodeisland," etc.

There was the preamble. It was followed by twenty-three articles divided into forty-one sections.

John Rutledge as chairman of the committee submitted these, and the clerk read them in his flat, toneless voice; but this was only a matter of form, for the delegates had copies of the thing right in their laps; and some of them, perhaps most of them, were aghast at what they saw.

The nomenclature was startling, though this did not in itself dismay. It was—*definite*. Gone were the lower-case "national legislature," "first branch," and "second branch"; they were replaced by "Congress," "House of Representatives," and "Senate." These terms were familiar enough, if not in this particular convention, for the youngest delegates had at least heard of the Stamp Act Congress and the First Continental Congress, while the Second Continental Congress still was doing business, with New York as a headquarters, and many of the delegates here were members of that body. In all of the states excepting New Jersey and Delaware the upper house was called the Senate, and in New Hampshire, Massachusetts, Pennsylvania, South Carolina, and Georgia the lower house was called the House of Representatives (in North Carolina it was the House of Commons; in Maryland and Virginia the House of Delegates; in New York, New Jersey, and Delaware the Assembly). Nor was it strange that the national executive should be declared the President of the United States, with the title, "His Excellency." The chief magistrates of Delaware, Pennsylvania, New Jersey, and New Hampshire were so designated, as was the presiding officer of the Continental Congress.

The members of the Committee of Detail had not exceeded their instructions as much as it at first appeared. Though they had added some, they had changed little. It did look awesome, · there in print, on paper, all those resolutions regularly assembled, numbered, split up: it frightened a man a bit to see the size of the central government that this instrument did indeed seem to set up. But the committee, though sometimes expanding a paragraph, or interpolating a clause from some other set, had not in fact reversed or even tampered much with the resolutions with which they had been entrusted.

By far the biggest change was in the section that defined the powers of Congress, and it was this that caused so much consternation. The convention here had been vague:

"Resolved, That the national legislature ought to possess the legislative rights vested in Congress by the Confederation; and moreover, to legislate in all cases for the general interests of the Union, and also in those to which the states are separately incompetent, or in which the harmony of the United States may be interrupted by the exercise of individual legislation."

The Committee of Detail would have none of that. The committee was well named. It specified, it enumerated, in Article VII:

"The legislature of the United States shall have the power to lay and collect taxes, duties, imposts and excises;

"To regulate commerce with foreign nations, and among the several states;

"To establish an uniform rule of naturalization throughout the United States;

"To coin money;

"To regulate the value of foreign coin;

"To fix the standard of weights and measures;

"To establish post offices;

"To borrow money, and emit bills on the credit of the United States;

"To appoint a treasurer by ballot;

"To constitute tribunals inferior to the Supreme Court;

"To make rules concerning captures on land and water;

"To declare the law and punishment of piracies and felonies committed on the high seas, and the punishment of counterfeiting the coin of the United States, and of offenses against the law of nations;

"To subdue a rebellion in any state, on the application of its legislature;

"To make war;

"To raise armies;

"To build and equip fleets;

"To call forth the aid of the militia, in order to execute

the laws of the Union, enforce treaties, suppress insurrections, and repel invasions;

"And to make all laws that shall be necessary and proper for carrying into execution the foregoing powers, and all other powers vested by this Constitution in the government of the United States, or in any department or office thereof."

This would be a quite different Congress from the one envisioned by most of the delegates.

There were six other sections to the momentous Article VII. Number 2 defined treason as "levying war against the United States, or any of them; and in adhering to the enemies of the United States, or any of them," and said that Congress could fix the penalty, though nobody could be convicted of treason "unless on the testimony of two witnesses." The third section set forth the three-fifths system of reckoning population for purposes of imposing taxes, being careful, of course, never to use that ugly word "slaves." Section 4 forbade an export tax, nor should any tax be laid "on the migration or importation of such persons as the several states shall think proper to admit; nor such migration or importation be prohibited." This was tossing a great deal into the lap of the South, and Charles Cotesworth Pinckney (who was back from Bethlehem) must have been pleased.

The remainder of the article read:

"Section 5. No capitation tax shall be laid, unless in proportion to the census hereinbefore directed to be taken.

"Section 6. No navigation act shall be passed without the assent of two-thirds of the members present in each house.

"Section 7. The United States shall not grant any title of nobility."

Here was a big mouthful, and it would take a long time chewing. A couple of delegates, perhaps stunned, moved that the convention adjourn for two days, until Wednesday, August 8, in order to give everybody a chance to study the report. Only Virginia, Maryland, and Pennsylvania favored this, and the motion was lost.

That Monday session did, however, adjourn until eleven

o'clock the following morning, as soon as the reading was finished, and without essaying to do any more business. As the delegates filed out, clutching their copies of the report, no doubt they were already resigned to the prospect of spending the rest of the summer away from home.

Chapter 19

Bit by Bit

PINCKNEY THE YOUNGER—it is hard to see why—started the Tuesday session with a motion that the report of the Committee of Detail be referred to the Committee of the Whole. The objections that this would be a waste of time were prompt and emphatic, and the motion was swamped; so that George Washington remained in the chairman's chair.

The preamble and the first and second articles were accepted without argument. The articles read: "I. The style of this government shall be, 'The United States of America' " and "2. The Government shall consist of supreme legislative, executive, and judicial powers."

The third article took a little longer. It read:

"The legislative power shall be vested in a Congress, to consist of two separate and distinct bodies of men, a House of Representatives and a Senate; each of which shall in all cases have a negative on the other. The legislature shall meet on the first Monday in December in every year."

Gouverneur Morris wanted to insert "legislative acts" for "all cases," and after scant discussion this lost in a tie vote.

Madison moved to strike out "each of which shall in all cases have a negative on the other." He said that this was implicit in the first part of the article, and hence unnecessary here. This motion was carried.

Madison also objected to setting a date for the meeting of the Congress, and here he raised a small storm. Morris and Pinckney agreed, but Gorham did not. Gorham said that setting a date would give the states a chance to pitch their own elections accordingly. It was a system in use in New England for many years, he said, and it had worked well. Ellsworth agreed with him, and so did Wilson. Rufus King could see no need for having a session of Congress every year. "A great vice of our system is that of legislating too much." Most of the law-making would be done by the states, the national legislature being concerned chiefly with matters of commerce and revenue. Randolph moved that the words "unless a different day shall be appointed by law" be appended to the article, and this was done.

Morris moved to have "December" changed to "May." Much of the business of Congress might be synchronized with or at least influenced by certain governmental and military measures taken in Europe, he said, and such measures are usually taken in the winter, the news of them reaching America in the spring. Also, December was such a nasty month in which to travel. On the other hand, it was pointed out to him, the winter is the best time in which to get business done. The motion was defeated.

It was voted to insert the words "once at least every year," and then the convention pushed on to Article IV.

Article IV presented more problems. It was a long one, seven sections, and all to do with the House of Representatives. The first section read:

"The members of the House of Representatives shall be chosen every second year, by the people of the several States comprehended within this Union. The qualifications of the electors shall be the same, from time to time, as those of the electors in the several States, of the most numerous branch of their own legislatures."

The committeemen had pondered long over that second sentence. About one-fifth of the adult white male residents of the thirteen states were not qualified to vote. Each state had different citizenship requirements, generally concerned with

length of residence. Maryland and Virginia excluded free
Negroes. In Pennsylvania, Georgia, and New Hampshire any
taxpayer could vote. The minimum age, twenty-one, was the
same in each state, but this was almost the only suffrage stipula-
tion that was. Most states had a property requirement, in some
cases real property only, in other cases either real or personal
property: New Jersey, for instance, insisted that before he could
vote a man must have land or goods worth fifty pounds.

For the federal government suddenly to impose its own
voting regulations on all the states alike would have caused
great confusion and no doubt resentment as well. It could have
imperiled the constitution's chances of ratification. In the circumstances the members of the Committee of Detail had
thought it best to leave this matter to the states.

Nevertheless, the section had no sooner been read aloud
than Gouverneur Morris was on his feet with a proposal that the
second sentence be struck out in order to substitute a clause
that would restrict the suffrage to freeholders—that is, owners of
real estate.

Madison in a carefully prepared speech backed this move,
and there were a few others, but many more voices were raised
in dissent. Land was hardly the right yardstick, if any yardstick
at all was needed. Probably nine-tenths of the residents of the
country were farmers, but what about the sons of farmers?
Would they have to abstain from voting until they had inherited? And what about the hard-working, respectable artisan
in the cities? Did he not deserve a vote? There were merchants
like Robert Morris here, like Elbridge Gerry, who could be
called rich, but they owned no land. Would *they* be disen-
franchised? On the other hand, if personalty were the standard,
what about great landowners like Washington, Jefferson, Madison, Monroe, who yet were in debt? For among the planters of
the South, as among those in the British West Indies, debt was
the customary state of affairs: it was taken for granted.

It was pointed out—by Madison himself, among others—
that the land situation would not stay the same forever. As the
population grew, the proportionate farm population would

shrink. The men in the west, the wild men whom the delegates at the convention feared, might not own anything else but they did own land; and the men of the Atlantic seaboard would tend more and more to become shipbuilders, mechanics, shopkeepers —non-landholding occupations all.

Benjamin Franklin mildly reminded the delegates that the common man should not be oppressed, for acres alone do not inculcate wisdom.

Morris's motion was overwhelmingly defeated, and the first section was passed as reported.

"Section 2. Every member of the House of Representatives shall be of the age of twenty-five years at least; shall have been a citizen of the United States for at least three years before his election; and shall be, at the time of his election, a resident of the state in which he shall be chosen."

Colonel Mason was all for opening the door wide for emigrants, but he did not want them making our laws for us. Three years wasn't long enough. He moved that it be changed to seven. Gouverneur Morris seconded this; and all the states but Connecticut voted for it.

Then Roger Sherman moved that the word "inhabitant" be substituted for the word "resident," and this caused an amazing amount of discussion, none of it important. It was finally accepted, unanimously.

Section 3 provided for a House of sixty-five, the seats being alloted according to the agreement previously reached. The Pinckneys asked that South Carolina be given six seats instead of five, but this was denied.

Section 4 *looked* innocuous. It took cognizance of the fact that populations might grow, that states might split or unite, and that new states would come into the union, and empowered Congress to "regulate the number of representatives by the number of inhabitants, according to the provisions hereinafter made, at the rate of one for every forty thousand."

Dr. Williamson moved to strike out the words "according to the provisions hereinafter made" and insert in their place "according to the rule hereafter to be provided for direct taxes."

Only Delaware dissented; but after the vote Rufus King was on his feet to demand what influence this was meant to have on the succeeding part of the report concerning the admission of slaves into the rule of representation. He hated slavery, and he made this amply clear.

Sherman tried to soothe him. The slave trade was "iniquitous," granted, but Sherman didn't think himself obliged to oppose it, "especially as the present article as amended did not preclude any arrangement whatever on that point in another place of the Report."

Sherman and Madison moved to insert the words "not exceeding" before the words "one for every forty thousand," and this was accepted.

Now Gouverneur Morris rose to move that the word "free" be inserted before the word "inhabitants"; and the fat was in the fire.

King's speech had been mild, compared with that of Morris. Slavery was "a nefarious institution," he stormed. It was "the curse of heaven." It had made a desert of the states where it was allowed.

"Upon what principle is it that the slaves shall be computed in the representation? Are they men? Then make them citizens and let them vote. Are they property? Why then is no other property included?"

As King had been, and rather more so, he was outspoken.

"I would sooner submit myself to a tax for paying for all the Negroes in the United States than saddle posterity with such a constitution," was the way he finished.

Nobody sent a challenge to Morris or to King, but surely those speeches rankled in southern hearts. More, they served notice on the South that because a compromise on slavery had been tentatively reached, this did not mean that everybody in the North approved it or would tolerate it.

Again there were those who sought to soothe the speaker, and only New Jersey voted for his motion, but the atmosphere was tense, the air electric, as before a tempest.

John Dickinson, who hailed from Delaware, moved that

the words "provided that each State shall have one representative at least" be added to the section; and this was done.

The convention moved hastily on to Section 5.

This called for the origin of all appropriation bills in the lower house, and it did not detain the delegates long—*this* day. A motion to strike it out as unnecessary was discussed pro and con briefly, and then passed. The next morning, however, both Randolph and Williamson gave notice of their intention to call for reconsideration of this section. At the same time Wilson served notice that he would call for a reconsideration of the seven-years-a-citizen amendment to Article IV, Section 2.

Sections 6 and 7 were accepted *nem. con.* The one provided that the House should have the sole power of impeachment and should choose its own speaker and other officers, and the second provided that vacancies should be supplied by writs of election from the executive authority of the state in which they occurred.

Article V had to do with the Senate, and the convention took it up with the same unquenchable determination to throw light into every corner of it. The heat of the day, the dreariness of the debates, the fact that it was now the second week of August, did not discourage them. They had a job, and they were going to do it.

There were four sections, and the first said, among other things, that vacancies be filled by the executives of the states. Wilson objected to this, and his objection provoked another spate of words. At one time in the course of this debate the whole convention was rocked yet again. Randolph of Virginia had asked for postponement of the final clause, "Each member shall have one vote," because, he said, the clause in the previous article that provided that money bills should originate in the House was about to be considered. If that clause was not reinstated, Randolph warned, he would move to call for reconsideration of the voting make-up of the Senate. *That* again? But his motion was adjudged improper, and the section was kept, albeit in slightly altered form.

Section 2 set a Senator's term at six years and arranged for a two-year stagger plan. It met no opposition.

Gouverneur Morris moved to change Section 3 so as to demand of a Senator fourteen years of citizenship, rather than the four set forth.

Practically everybody had something to say about this, and they were fervent. In time it was voted out, and Morris promptly moved to make it thirteen years. When this was downed, General Pinckney tried ten years, and lost. Nine was at last agreed to.

There was no argument about Section 4, which simply stated that the Senate should choose its own president and other officers.

Chapter 20

Mr. Fitch's Chug-Chug

THERE WAS an interesting interruption to the work the morning of August 22 when the delegates turned out in a body at the invitation of a group of local businessmen who were backing an inventor named John Fitch, to watch a test of Fitch's "steam-boat."

It was a lovely day, and the Delaware sparkled. There was a large crowd, including every one of the twenty-one backers, Philadelphia merchants most of them, though there was a hatter; two physicians; the Geographer-General of the new republic, Thomas Hutchins; and Israel Israel, the proprietor of a pub, the Cross Keys, at the corner of Third and Chestnut Streets.

Fitch had devised the driving mechanism while nursing a hangover, of all times; and conceivably the contraption itself showed this. There were six oars on each side, propelled in the manner of canoe paddles, five and a half feet each stroke, by rods that were driven by an axle tree on a wheel eighteen inches in diameter. The wheel in turn was driven by the second steam engine ever built in America (though two others had been brought over from England). It was noisy, and it was smoky, but it worked. Undeniably it worked. With Fitch himself and his partner, an ebullient, ingenious young watchmaker named Henry Voight, at the controls, the craft actually forged *upstream,* against the current, at a speed estimated by some to be as fast as two miles an hour. A great cheer arose.

George Washington did not attend that particular party, but of course Benjamin Franklin was there, for he was always interested in anything new; and had any of the delegates remarked that after all two miles an hour was not going to offer any competition to the poled Durham boats commonly used in the Delaware, so what good was the thing? the sage could have made him a pat answer. Some years before, when Franklin was United States Ambassador to France, he and many others had watched an earlier exhibition of a new invention, in this case a manned balloon. The bag did not go up high and did not stay up long, but the ascent, like Fitch's steamboat on that August morning in Philadelphia, was a success. "But of what use is the thing?" somebody said to Franklin afterward. "Of what use is a newborn babe?" the sage replied.

The outing was a pleasant exception, for most of the convention's days, as August ground on, were almost indescribably dull. There remained a certain tartness of temper, and though the big-states-versus-small-states fire had been extinguished, the North-South volcano remained, a volcano that smoked only languidly but was litten from time to time by bright, ominous flames.

Their opinions of one another they kept to themselves perforce, but their opinion of the men who would sometime operate this machine that they were building, the future senators and representatives, was abundantly clear. They didn't trust them. They tried to plug up every possible loophole in advance. They had been that way from the beginning, but the attitude—perhaps the weather had something to do with it?—was intensified as the convention continued.

The most fretful and suspicious were Gerry, Mason, and Randolph, who were known by many of the others—though not to their faces—as the Committee of Fear and Apprehension. But there were others almost as bad.

Rutledge complained from the floor one day of the "tediousness of the proceedings," and Ellsworth warmly agreed: "We grow more and more skeptical as we proceed. If we do not decide soon, we shall be unable to come to any decision." The next day Rutledge brought in a motion that all sessions start promptly at 10:00 A.M. and continue until 4:00 P.M., and that no motion for adjournment before that hour should be accepted. This was passed, 8 to 2.

Having dispensed with the two houses of Congress separately, the convention now took them up together. Article VI was a long one, thirteen sections, but these for the most part had to do with procedural details—quorums, journals, immunity to arrest, etc. The convention treated each as though the whole future of the republic hung upon it, taking the better part of a week over that one article, though in the end almost nothing had been accomplished.

For instance, Section 10 provided that "The members of each House shall receive a compensation for their services, to be ascertained and paid by the State in which they shall be chosen." When it was pointed out that this would work against the states farther away, the section was changed to read that the Congressmen be paid out of the national treasury. Ellsworth wished to go further. He thought that the *amount* of pay should be put down into print, and he threw out that this might be five dollars a day while actually on the job and five dollars for every thirty miles of traveling to and from. Caleb Strong thought this extravagant. Four dollars ought to be enough. Nothing was done about this.

Consideration of the article was interrupted from time to time by scheduled reconsideration of other articles. Wilson and Randolph moved that members of the House of Representatives be required to have lived only four years in the state from which they were elected, not seven years, as provided in the amended

Section 2 of Article IV. Williamson thought it ought to be nine years. Gerry believed that they all ought to be *native* Americans. The article at last was left untouched. A similar section of Article V called for Senators to be nine-year residents of their respective states, and an effort to have this changed to seven years was defeated.

Section 13 was the last of Article VI. It was also the longest, and more time was devoted to it than was devoted to any of the others. It had to do with the presidential negative. Madison made the only radical motion when he tried to put over a pet project of his—to have the judiciary share with the executive the privilege of "negativing" bills passed by Congress. This stimulated a lot of talk before it was voted down.

The only change made in the long section was to increase from two-thirds to three-fourths the majorities in both houses needed to repass anything over a negative and to give the President ten days (Sundays excepted) in which to make up his mind, instead of seven, as previously.

Article VII, with its long list of the duties and privileges and powers of Congress (*see* Chapter 19), was sure to take a long time, but its introduction found the delegates determined to step up the pace, if possible.

The very first power, "to lay and collect taxes, duties, imports, and excises," prompted the South again to ask whether this might possibly include a tax on exports, and to demand, again, that such a tax be specifically forbidden. There were some caustic remarks about this and about the slave trade. Nothing was done, but the hard feeling remained.

After that there were four quick ones, for which no more than a series of nods, not even a roll call, was needed.

When "To establish post-offices" came along, Elbridge Gerry moved to add "and post-roads," and this was done readily enough, without debate.

"To borrow money, and emit bills on the credit of the United States." The first part of this was all right, but the second part found the anti-paper money fanatics in full cry. Now and then a restrained voice was raised in defense of paper money, perhaps possibly maybe under certain careful restrictions, but the opposite side was much louder—and wordier. Read of Delaware even saw the offending phrase as "as alarming as the mark of the beast in Revelations." It was stricken out by a 9 to 2 vote.

There was a great deal of hair-splitting about the repression-of-privacy power, which was retained.

"To subdue a rebellion in any State, on the application of its legislature." There were many opinions here, all of them aired. Some men wanted to cut out the words "on the application of its legislature"; others wished to cut out the whole thing, for they thought that the federal government should never in any circumstances whatever invade any state with a military force: Shays' Rebellion would have been a lot bloodier than it was, Gerry avowed, if the federal troops had arrived. Still others would add "or the executive," or, after cutting out "its legislature," put in "its executive provided that the legislature is not in session." Gouverneur Morris tartly remarked that the governor in case might be *leading* the rebellion, and what then? but nobody paid much attention to this. Various other amendments were proposed and in some cases even adopted, but the final vote was a tie, so none of these stood and the power remained the same as it had been when reported out of committee.

"To make war" was changed to "To declare war."

"To raise armies" was changed to "To raise and support armies."

"To build and equip fleets" was changed to "To provide and maintain a navy."

Martin and Gerry, who shared with so many of their fellow countrymen a deep-seated horror of a standing army, moved that such an army, if it had to exist, should be limited to   men, adding that about 2,000 was what they had in mind for the blank space. The motion was defeated.

All of this took time, and the procedure was not hastened by the practice of some delegates to submit lists of matters that they thought the Committee of Detail should have considered and reported on. One morning Madison submitted nine of these and the younger Pinckney eleven, and two days later Pinckney (who must have been a busy man) submitted thirteen more, a sort of early Bill of Rights, while Gouverneur Morris submitted six, largely to do with presidential advisors, and Gerry submitted three of his own. Some of these were duplicates. All were turned over to the Committee of Detail.

The learned lawyers had a lot to say about the Statute of Edward III as expanded under Edward VI when Article VII, Section 2, came up. That section defined treason. Once again, there was a prodigious amount of talking, and even a motion to recommit the section, which motion was lost in a split vote.

ALEXANDER HAMILTON

A few words were shifted, here and there, and the whole thing was passed upon at last.

Alexander Hamilton, heeding that cry for help from his former chief, had striven to persuade either Yates or Lansing to go back to Philadelphia with him, so that New York would at least be represented, even if by an habitually divided vote. They both refused; and at last Hamilton had come back alone. He was still an accredited delegate. He could work "out of doors," the kind of work he liked best, and in which he excelled, and he could even take part in the debates, but he had no vote, since the New York legislature had given that state's delegation instructions that any vote in the convention must be cast by at least two of them. This put Hamilton in a baffling position, but he made the best of it. Naturally he was not appointed to the Grand Committee, which, under the chairmanship of Governor Livingston of New Jersey, was appointed to consider and report upon the proposition that the federal government pay the debts of the several states, and also the proposition that the federal government have charge of the state militias.

This group—it was sometimes called the Committee of Eleven—reported August 21. It recommended that Congress (the new one) be given power to pay the debts incurred by the Continental Congress as well as those "incurred by the States during the late war, for the common defence and general welfare." It recommended also that Congress be empowered to make laws for "organizing, arming and disciplining the Militia, and for governing such part of them as may be employed in the service of the United States, reserving to the States respectively the appointment of officers, and the authority of training the Militia according to the discipline prescribed by the United States."

These seemed harmless enough, though it was true that *anything* pertaining to money or militiamen was likely to raise a row; yet it was voted that they should "lie upon the table."

This made room for the explosion of that most explosive subject of them all—the slave trade.

Chapter 21

The "Peculiar Institution"

THESE MEN WERE conscious of their dignity. "Every member, rising to speak, shall address the President; and whilst he shall be speaking, none shall pass between them, or hold discourse with another, or read a book, pamphlet, or paper, printed or manuscript," was one of the first of their standing rules.

However, you cannot control the tone of a man's voice; and words, at the Constitutional Convention, were not subject to censor.

The vaporizing, testy Luther Martin was born to trouble and glad of it. He it was who touched off the slavery squabble when out of a clear sky he moved to vary Section 4 of Article VII in such a way as to allow a prohibition of or a tax on the importation of slaves. He said that word, "slaves." His own state of Maryland had recently forbidden the importation of slaves, though not slavery itself, and so had Virginia. Slavery, Martin said, weakened states. At the same time an increase of slaves would increase the chance of insurrection, and the northern states, by this constitution they were drawing up here, would then be obliged to go to the aid of the weaker southern states. What's more, he found it "inconsistent with the principles of the revolution and dishonorable to the American character to have such a feature in the Constitution."

About twenty per cent of the population of the United States at that time was slave. Massachusetts had prohibited slavery altogether, and all of the states excepting only the Carolinas and Georgia had prohibited the importation of slaves, always a dirty business. Maryland and Virginia didn't want any more blacks, didn't need them, and in fact were exporting slaves to South Carolina, where they were used in raising indigo and rice. The rice swamps in particular were hard on slaves, who died like flies there. Virginia could not supply enough replacements. If the African slave trade was prohibited, South Carolina —and this was true only to a slightly lesser extent of Georgia —would have her principle source of income cut off. North Carolina didn't care much, one way or the other.

Rutledge answered Martin. A fine, fierce, hawk-eyed, white-haired gentleman of the old school, he was scathing. He was not worried about slave insurrections, and he would gladly exempt the other states from their duty to protect South Carolina. But, sir, "Religion and humanity have nothing to do with this question. Interest alone is the governing principle with nations. The true question at present is whether the southern states shall or shall not be parties to the Union."

The Pinckneys too served blunt warning that South Carolina would not be a party to any instrument that might permit a tax on exports and might prohibit the trade in slaves. There wasn't the slightest doubt that they meant this.

A horror of slavery had been making itself felt all over the country, especially among religious groups, and abolitionist societies were springing up. Even a good part of the precotton South was at least indifferent, not defensive; and New Englanders and the Quakers of Pennsylvania seethed with indignation. Even while the convention was sitting in Philadelphia the Continental Congress in New York was at last settling the problem of the great Northwest Territory, comprising the states-to-be of Ohio, Illinois, Indiana, Michigan, and Wisconsin, and among other things it ordered that there should be no slavery in any of those places—ever. There was a general belief that if slavery could be kept from crossing the Alleghenies it was doomed: it would die of its own accord, it would wither on the vine. But this could not happen if seemingly endless reinforcements were pumped into its ranks from the bottomless Africa.

South Carolina's economic life was at stake, and she meant to fight. Georgia felt the same way.

The Connecticut leaders Ellsworth and Sherman tried to placate the others. Each despised the institution of slavery, but neither wished to see two states drop out of the Union. Also, they were eager to see the convention get its work done.

The most fiery antislavery speech of all was made by a southerner, George Mason.

British merchants, he stormed, had foisted "this infernal trade" upon America, and Britons had balked every attempt on the part of Virginia to eliminate it.

"Slavery discourages arts and manufactures. The poor despise labor when performed by slaves. They prevent the immigration of whites, who really enrich and strengthen a country. They produce the most pernicious effect on manners. Every master of slaves is born a petty tyrant. They bring the judgement of heaven on a country. As nations can not be rewarded or punished in the next world they must be in this. By an inevitable chain of causes and effects providence punishes national sins by national calamities."

Colonel Mason himself was an owner of slaves. But he said that he "held it essential" that the central government had the power to prevent an increase of slavery.

Finally he took a swipe at the Yankee shipowners and skippers who were growing rich in the slave trade: "some of our Eastern brethren . . . embarked in this nefarious traffic."

"Let us not intermeddle," pleaded Ellsworth. "As population increases, poor laborers will be so plentiful as to render slaves useless. Slavery in time will not be a speck in our country."

There was much more, and it was as bitter as gallwood, until at last Gouverneur Morris moved that the whole subject— slaves, export taxes, and a navigation act—be put into the hands of the all-states committee.

This was done, with only New Hampshire, Pennsylvania, and Delaware voting against it.

What they did with the day during which the Committee

of Eleven deliberated hardly mattered in the context of the convention as a whole. There were always details to be ironed out, small matters to be checked. But all of this work might be wasted if some compromise wasn't reached.

The committee reported back Friday, August 24, through its chairman, Governor Livingston. It recommended the substitution for that part of the fourth section as was referred to it, of: "The migration or importation of such persons as the several States now existing shall think proper to admit, shall not be prohibited by the Legislature prior to the year 1800, but a tax or duty may be imposed on such migration or importation at a rate not exceeding the average of the duties laid on imports."

That word "migration" was ironic to any who knew about the nature of the slave trade, which was beastly, but a clear attempt had been made to look both ways, and the phrase "the several States now existing" neatly mitigated against a jump of slavery across the mountains.

The report also recommended that Section 5, which prohibited a head tax "unless in proportion to the Census hereinbefore directed to be taken," be stricken out, a victory for the South, and that Section 6, which called for a two-thirds vote in each house for the passage of any navigation act, be thrown out, a victory for the North.

General Pinckney moved to strike out the words "the year eighteen hundred" and to insert "the year eighteen hundred and eight."

Why he did this—what difference eight years would be expected to make—is not clear. What is significant is that the motion was promptly seconded by Judge Gorham, a New Englander, and that after only a few disparaging remarks on the part of James Madison, a slave owner and pronounced antislavery man, it was voted in, 7 to 4, the dissenters being New Jersey, Pennsylvania, Delaware—and Virginia.

Gouverneur Morris favored making the clause read: "importation of slaves into North Carolina, South Carolina and Georgia shall not be prohibited," etc. He wasn't trying to be sarcastic, only to be clear. But if his language was objectionable to any of the delegates from any of those states he would not press it.

Colonel Mason was not opposed to using the horrid word "slaves," but he did oppose the naming of the three states, for he feared that some of their people might take offense.

Sherman liked Morris's words better than those of the clause they had just voted in, and Clymer of Pennsylvania concurred with him.

Dr. Williamson of North Carolina said that he personally was against slavery, but he thought it better to let South Carolina and Georgia in on those terms than to exclude them altogether.

Morris withdrew his motion.

John Dickinson, an austere, ascetic personage of Quaker leanings, moved to make the clause read: "The importation of slaves into such of the States as shall permit the same shall not be prohibited by the Legislature of the United States until the year 1808," but this was much too outspoken for the delegates, who voted it down unanimously.

As to the second clause, Baldwin moved to strike out "average of the duties laid on imports" and to insert "common impost on articles not enumerated." This was done, with no discussion.

Sherman deplored this second clause as acknowledging men to be property. Langdon and King both said that they assumed that this was the price of the first part. General Pinckney said that of course it was.

"Not to tax," Colonel Mason said, "would be equivalent to a bounty on the importation of slaves."

Madison too regretted that it should be confessed in the Constitution that there was property in men.

It was at last agreed, without objection, to make the clause read "but a tax or duty may be imposed on such importation not exceeding ten dollars for each person," and then the second part as amended was agreed to.

The head-tax section was agreed to with no voice raised against it.

Consideration of the section dealing with a two-thirds vote for any navigation act, was postponed.

The crisis was past. Nobody was pleased, and many of the men were ashamed of what they had just done, but at least the convention was still in business.

Chapter 22

"The Best We Could Get"

NOBODY, LEAST OF ALL the delegates themselves, had expected the convention to go on like this, and as they entered September, the rumors outside flew fast and furious.

On September 5 there was a scene of some slight embarrassment downstairs in the Pennsylvania State House. The state's one legislative body had adjourned the previous March until this very day, a Wednesday. Now they were reconvening, according to schedule, only to find that their quarters were taken.

Everybody was very polite. The federal people assured the state people that they would hardly be there many more days, they were sorry; and the state people bowed and said that was quite all right and take your time, gentlemen, after which they bowed again and went upstairs to hold their session there.

In truth it had been a trying time—the weather, scorching hot, didn't help—and the wonder was that the men downstairs had kept their tempers as well as they did. Luther Martin hadn't kept his. Just the previous day he had left, spewing expletives, and right now, back in Baltimore, he was preparing his report to the Maryland legislature—a report in which he blasted the Constitutional Convention for exceeding its instructions and misbehaving in a multitude of other ways. They were well rid of him.

The days of wrangling and of crisis were gone, but there remained a very great deal to be done, and it was wearying work. There were so many ends to tuck in! so many loose bits to tighten! The matter of the Supreme Court they had handled with dispatch, and without acrimony, but the matter of the President, his rights, his powers, most of all the manner in which he should be elected, had given and was still to give them many a trying hour. Every delegate seemed to have his own opinion on every phase of the Presidency, and virtually every one of them spoke up.

Only the previous day, the day Martin stamped out, the convention had at last agreed, by no means unanimously, that treaties with foreign nations should be made not by the Senate, as the article had for some time stood, but by the President with the advice and consent of the Senate, a vote of two-thirds being called for.

Only the previous day, again, it had been decided, unanimously this time, to give Congress "exclusive Legislation" over any district "not exceeding ten Miles square" which might be given to it by one or several of the states as a national capital. There were those who pooh-poohed this as too grandiose—*one* square mile would surely be enough to take care of all the future needs of the central government, several said—but there had been no snapping.

One of the most important of all their decisions in this period had been made readily enough, smoothly. This was a resolution on how the completed constitution—if it ever *was* completed—should be submitted to the states, or to the people, for their approval. It was decided that the Continental Congress should be notified, though it was not proposed to demand of this flabby body that it vote itself out of existence: that would be going too far. Copies of the document-to-be would be sent to the various state legislatures with a request that they call state conventions for the purpose of ratification—or refusal to ratify. When nine of the states had ratified it, the constitution would go into effect. Here was the nut of the problem. The others could string along later, if they wished, but the constitution would *start* as soon as the ninth state convention had endorsed it.

Anywhere else in the world this would have been called a *coup d'état*. It was a strictly illegal act; but then, the Continental Congress was an illegal body in the first place, so where would be the harm in replacing it with a *stronger* illegal body? There were a few mild reminders that the Articles of Confederation called for unanimity of amendment and that *they* had not become effective until the thirteenth state had agreed—Maryland had taken four years to ratify them—but this was brushed aside.

It really began to look near, that long-longed-for final adjournment, when on September 8, which was a Saturday, the convention appointed a Committee of Style, charged with whipping the whole thing into more acceptable shape. The committee consisted of Samuel Johnson of Connecticut, Alexander Hamilton, Gouverneur Morris, Rufus King, and James Madison. Judge Johnson was the chairman.

In a day when letter-writing was a common accomplishment, letters being, in effect, the newspapers, a man's literary manners and mannerisms, his directness, his way with words, were things about him that his acquaintances knew as well as they knew his walk, his hiccup, his face, and often even better. Of this quintet there was one outstanding stylist, Morris. It was believed by everybody that Judge Johnson would assign Morris to the writing task itself, and this was done, though of course they all had a part in saying what would be written, and how it would be arranged, and indeed a sixth, James Wilson, was called in at least once for consultation.

The convention met Monday, the tenth, but since the committee wasn't ready for it, it droned on with other, sweep-up subjects.

Mason, Pinckney, and a few others wanted a bill of rights to be incorporated into the constitution itself before it was too late. There had been some previous talk of this, but the advocates of the plan had no organization, no drive. Most of the delegates simply couldn't see any sense to stipulating that the freedom of the press must not be threatened or that troops may not be quartered on private citizens in peacetime. All of that could be assumed, they said. When it came to a vote they prevailed, and not one state went on record as favoring any sort of bill of rights.

Tuesday, September 11, the convention was called to order, but there was no business ready for it, for the Committee of Style was not yet prepared to report, so it adjourned until the following morning.

The committee *was* ready then.

Long-winded on the floor, Gouverneur Morris was admirably terse when he took pen in hand. He and the other members of the Committee of Style had reduced the ungainly mass of material that had been turned over to them from twenty-three articles to seven. They had supplied also a preamble:

"We the people of the United States, in Order to form a more perfect Union, establish Justice, insure domestic Tranquility, provide for the common defence, promote the general Welfare, and secure the Blessings of Liberty to ourselves and our Posterity, do ordain and establish this Constitution for the United States of America."

That is a fine phrase: "We the people of the United States . . ." It challenges. It is arresting. It is much more vivid than what it replaced: "We the people of New Hampshire, Massachusetts, etc." Yet it was not put there for its dramatic effect, as it might have been, but for the sake of accuracy. Until a few days before it had not occurred to many delegates that the constitution could be effective unless and until ratified by all of the states, as was the case with the Articles of Confederation. Stipulating that nine would be enough was a last-minute, and radical, idea. Supposing only that nine or ten or eleven or even twelve of the states did ratify it, then having all thirteen posted on the masthead would look a little foolish, and for a time at least—conceivably forever—would be untrue. So "the United States" was substituted, with stunning effect.

With this report the committee submitted a letter it was suggested be sent to the Continental Congress along with copies of the constitution itself as finally agreed upon. The letter was neither imperious nor humble. "That it (the constitution) will meet the full and entire approbation of every State is not perhaps to be expected," was the way it ended, "but each will doubtless consider, that had her interest alone been consulted, the consequences might have been particularly disagreeable or injurious to others; that it is liable to as few exceptions as could reasonably have been expected, we hope and believe; that it may promote the lasting welfare of that country so dear to us all, and secure her freedom and happiness, is our most ardent wish."

The delegates spent the rest of that week going over both letter and constitution paragraph by paragraph, almost word by word. In general they liked what they read, and objections were few and brief. The constitution as we know it today is virtually the same as that brought in by the Committee of Style.

There was another attempt—and it resulted in another failure—to get some bill-of-rights provisions written into it. There were some trifling changes, changes of words rather than of fact or meaning.

One last-minute change was supported, unexpectedly, from the chair. It was to make 30,000 persons the unit of population for electing members of the House of Representatives. George Washington himself said that he thought that this should be done, the only time he had ever spoken from the floor as a delegate. It *was* done, of course, unanimously.

It was ordered that a copy of the constitution be engrossed for a formal signing.

Not everybody was delighted with this document. Hamilton and Charles Pinckney both found grave faults in it, but each said that he would not only sign it but would work for its ratification in his state.

That was the general attitude: It isn't very good, but it's the best we can get.

Others had decided not to sign, and three of these—Mason, Randolph, and Gerry—announced their decisions from the floor, giving their reasons.

Mason objected chiefly to the fact that there was no anti-slavery clause, but he feared too a central government which could enact navigation laws by a simple majority—feared, that is, for the future of his beloved South.

Randolph was a politician with his ear to the ground, as everyone immediately saw. He was still in his thirties, handsome, of good family, ambitious, and with the gift of gab. He truly did not believe that the constitution as written would be ratified, and he was reluctant to have his name associated with a losing cause. On the other hand, he did not wish to appear unpatriotic. He refused to say whether he would support the constitution at the Virginia ratification convention. He didn't know that yet, though he knew that he would not sign it. He wanted to see, first, which way the cat would jump. He did not say this in so many words, but he didn't need to. For this behavior his stout colleague George Mason was to call him "Little Arnold"—meaning a small Benedict Arnold—for the rest of his life.

Gerry's reasons were more mixed. Most of the objections he voiced were absurdly petty. Throughout the convention Elbridge Gerry had objected to almost everything that he had not himself proposed. He was a great objector, to the last.

Benjamin Franklin, always the conciliator, asked James Wilson to read a statement for him.

"Mr. President: I confess that there are several parts of this constitution which I do not at present approve, but I am not sure that I shall never approve them . . ." His plea was for understanding of the other man's point of view. He told a story of Steele, who in a dedication addressed to the Pope pointed out "that the only difference between our Churches in the opinion of the certainty of their doctrines is, that the Church of Rome is infallible and the Church of England is never in the wrong." Franklin always did have a story to illustrate and enliven a point. He finished:

"On the whole, Sir, I cannot help expressing a wish that every member of the Convention who may still have objections to it, would with me, on this occasion, doubt a little of his own

THE SIGNING OF THE CONSTITUTION

infallibility—and to make manifest our unanimity, put his name to this instrument."

It was a telling address, and it won over several doubters, including Gouverneur Morris, who before that time had meant to refuse to sign.

The same Gouverneur Morris it was who that night at a meeting of the Pennsylvania delegates at Franklin's home proposed that the statement "Done in Convention by the Unanimous Consent of the States present, etc.," which would be strictly true, be put above the signatures. The public should not know that they had wavered.

This was done. The actual signing—and it was the only business of the day—was done in the same State House room, without any notable ceremony, on Monday, September 17.

The hot spell had been broken, and it was a clear, pleasantly cool day.

After that the members of the Pennsylvania legislature were permitted to come downstairs and again occupy their usual quarters, while the delegates of the Constitutional Convention went over to the City Tavern, on Second Street near Walnut, for a bang-up farewell dinner.

The next day those ex-delegates started home for the biggest fight of all—the fight for ratification.

Chapter 23

The Home Stretch

AT THE OUTBREAK of the Revolution it was estimated that about a third of the Americans were in favor of independence, a third were loyal to the throne, and a third didn't gave a damn one way or the other.

It was not so when the new Constitution was presented to the people. Then they promptly broke into Federalists, those who favored it, and Antifederalists, those opposed. Precious few were indifferent, and feeling ran high.

Dunlap & Claypoole, the Philadelphia printers, were turning them out as fast as they could, and copies were being sent to all parts of the country as well as to Europe, where they created much excitement in parliamentary circles.

The Antifederalists were not organized—they never were to be—but they existed even before the Constitution was made public. There were thousands who had been leery of that convention in Philadelphia, shrouded as it was in four months of secrecy, and were prepared to dislike *anything* that came out of it.

The Federalists were men like those who had in fact framed the Constitution, men who believed that unless the nation got a strong central government, and got it fast, it faced anarchy.

They were moneyed men, for the most part, interested,

understandably, in protecting their money. An exception was the Hudson River Valley aristocracy, the great upstate patroons, who to a man were Antifederalist. Unlike the planters of the South, who were usually in debt, these landowners had huge incomes in the form of rents, and thanks to the tariff charged at the port of New York they were taxed but lightly. They wanted it to stay that way.

The Federalists were, generally, city men, the Antifederalists farmers. The Federalists were professional men, doctors, lawyers, ministers, and also artisans and merchants. The Antifederalists were soft-money men, debtors.

Not all of the Antifederalists were as George Washington saw them, small-time politicians who feared to lose their jobs if a great federal government overshadowed the governments of the states. Many were sincere believers in states' rights, who thought that the scheme put forward by the Philadelphia men was not only illegal but dangerous, even monstrous.

The Federalists had more leaders and better leaders, "names" like Washington, Franklin, Madison, Hamilton, but the Antifederalists, though on the whole not so articulate, still included some great men—George Mason, Patrick Henry, George Clinton, Richard Henry Lee.

Some of the Antifederalists' arguments took the Federalists by surprise. The states'-rights cry was of course expected, as was the drifting-into-monarchy wail, but not many of the delegates had been prepared for the to-do about the absence of a bill of rights, and none had even dreamed that the idea of ten square miles of stateless capital would be used as a bogey to frighten the back-country voters.

Time after time exasperated Federalist orators pointed out that the right of assemblage and a free press and so forth did not need to be mentioned in the Constitution, since all rights already invested in the individual states remained there unless specifically expunged. It did no good. Thousands went on believing that this new Constitution was an instrument of tyranny. It was even said that it was meant to do away with trial by jury —nonsense, to be sure, but nonsense that had a telling effect.

The fuss about the national capital was even sillier, but quite as powerful. That capital was pictured as a walled fortress from which sallies could be made—literally!—upon the surrounding countryside, which in time would all be subdued. It was pictured as a stronghold of tyranny, a mighty fastness of iniquity, to which all sinners and malcontents would flock. It cost the Federalists a great many votes.

Philadelphia had its eye on that capital-to-be, and the Philadelphia Federalists were eager to have their state be the first to ratify the Constitution, which they believed would greatly strengthen their chances of getting the prize. They were perhaps *too* eager. There was something suspicious about their avidity—or, at least, so said the Antifederalists.

The Federalists actually tried to jam through the Pennsylvania legislature a bill offering to donate those ten square miles somewhere near Philadelphia before the Continental Congress had even started to debate on the Constitution.

That debate took place, in New York, September 26 and 27. Ten of the convention delegates were in Congress, almost a third of the total, and these with their supporters tried hard to get an unqualified endorsement of the Constitution. But this was not to be. The best they could do was a no-comment assignment to the various states.

That was the first hurdle.

The news reached Philadelphia the morning of September 29, and the Federalist members of the Assembly immediately demanded that a date be fixed for the state ratification convention. The Antifederalists protested that they wanted more time. They stayed away from the State House, where the Federalists found themselves two short of a quorum. They descended in force upon the homes of the two nearest Antifederalists, hauled these wretches to the State House, sat them down, and kept them there until the Assembly could with all due propriety issue a call for a state convention to be held in November.

It was to be the classic pattern: the frontier against the seaboard, upstate against the metropolis, west against east, backwoodsmen against city slickers.

In this case the Antifederalists of the western counties protested bitterly and long that the convention was held too soon
for them. They never had a chance, they cried. For years afterward they were to contend that they'd been robbed.

The convention that did assemble was undoubtedly
weighted for the Federalists, who, a little alarmed by the rage
of their opponents, graciously consented to allow those opponents to talk as often and as long as they wished. The convention lasted from November 21 to December 12, and when at last
a vote was taken the Federalists were shown to have almost
twice as many, 43 to 23.

Even so, Pennsylvania was not the first state to ratify. A few
days before, December 7, a convention in Delaware had quietly
—and unanimously—voted for the new Constitution.

On December 18 New Jersey ratified, and on January 2,
1788, Georgia did. Both of these votes were unanimous. (The
word, however, should not be taken literally. It is unlikely that
every single convention delegate in Delaware, New Jersey, and
Georgia favored the Constitution. Announcing a "unanimous"
vote was a custom of the time, to which the losers customarily
consented. It fooled nobody, but it was somehow thought to be
proper.)

Connecticut was a sobersided state, and could be counted
on the side of the angels, so nobody gasped when Connecticut
voted 128 to 40 at Hartford on January 9 for the Constitution.

The great debate was on. In all manner of huts and houses
and shops men argued. Men shook their fists. Men wrote letters
to the newspapers.

In New York the first flood of Antifederalist literature was
particularly heavy, for New York had been prepared for the
fight against the Constitution. Lansing and Yates, quitting early
and coming home, had not kept their mouths shut, and to the
top men of the Clinton machine the Constitution, when at last
it was published, came as no stunning shock. Alexander Hamilton decided to reply in kind, and he persuaded John Jay and
James Madison, who was in New York as a member of the Continental Congress, to co-operate with him in a series of letters

addressed to the people of New York State and setting forth, clearly, lucidly, in a thought-out order, the advantages of the new Constitution. They got William Duer to do a few too, but these were not printed with the others. They also approached Gouverneur Morris, but he was in Philadelphia.

There were eighty-five of these papers, almost two-thirds of them by Hamilton, and they appeared two or three or sometimes even four times a week in four different New York City newspapers between October and March. They were widely reprinted elsewhere. They were all signed "Publius," but everybody knew who had written them. On March 22, in New York, the first thirty-six were published in book form as *The Federalist,* and on May 28 the rest were similarly published.

The Federalist papers were written hastily, though not heatedly, and they were meant to be no more than political pamphlets. Posterity has hailed them as a literary masterpiece. How many votes they swayed, if any, will never be known.

The Constitution suffered its first setback in mid-February when a New Hampshire convention that was heavily Antifederalist met at Exeter. Knowing this imbalance, and seeing that many of the Antifederalist delegates were badly informed, or misinformed, the Federalists fought for and eventually got, by a 56-to-51 vote, an indefinite adjournment.

This shook the true believers. Washington, back among his buckwheat at Mount Vernon, wrote to Henry Knox, to Benjamin Lincoln, to Caleb Gibbs, and to John Langdon, all New Englanders, that he feared that it would have a big and a bad influence on the forthcoming convention in Virginia.

In Rhode Island the following months the Constitution was severely beaten, but there the circumstances were unusual. The legislature refused to call a convention, as requested by the Continental Congress, but instead had the towns polled on the question of whether or not *to* hold such a convention. Rhode Island undoubtedly was Antifederalist, but the result—twenty-two towns opposed to a convention, only two in favor of it— was hardly indicative of the split. Federalists, protesting that the poll was illegal, stayed away in droves. In Newport, the state's largest city, for instance, only eleven Federalists voted; and in Providence there was only *one*.

The Massachusetts convention was by far the largest. There were 355 delegates, and the meeting was held in Boston in February. Everybody knew that it was going to be close.

Shays' Rebellion was a year back, and all had been forgiven. Eighteen to twenty of the men who had taken part in it —on Shays' side, that is—were among the delegates. As debtors, they were all opposed to the Constitution.

The delegates from the Maine counties too were against it. For years they had been trying to achieve separate statehood, and they were near it now and feared that a strong federal government would spoil their chances.

Of the four national delegates from Massachusetts, Judge Gorham, Caleb Strong, and Rufus King attended the Boston convention and spoke in favor of the Constitution they had signed. Elbridge Gerry was invited, but he sulked.

Ex-Governor Bowdoin was in favor of the Constitution.

Two more important figures in Massachusetts politics, Samuel Adams and John Hancock—John Adams was abroad— were not sure of themselves. Adams, perhaps senile, shifted back and forth. He could have killed the thing, or he could have caused it to be carried. He did neither.

Hancock was different. A very rich man—inherited—he was as vain as a peacock ("King John" they used to call him in Philadelphia when he was president of the Continental Congress, as much for his majestical mannerisms as for the size and splendor of his entourage), he had never recovered from the disappointment he felt when George Washington and not himself had been appointed commander-in-chief of the Continental Army. Hancock was now governor of Massachusetts, and at the height of his popularity there. He had been named president of the convention, but he pleaded off attendance on account of gout. He wanted to see which way it would go before he got involved.

An informal delegation of politicians headed by Rufus King called on Governor Hancock and informed him that they had it on good authority that the Constitution would be defeated in Virginia. This meant that George Washington couldn't be the first President of the United States. It also meant that that President would surely come from Massachusetts, the second largest state, and who would fill the bill better than John Hancock?

From that moment Hancock became an ardent supporter of the Constitution. He forgot his gout and went to the convention hall to preside.

It was a very serious, even a solemn convention, and it ended with a close vote: 187 ayes, 168 nays. The Constitution had squeaked through.

The vote was better in Maryland, the first southern state, April 28. It was, despite the efforts of the perfervid Luther Martin, 63 to 11.

In South Carolina, May 23, it was 149 to 73.

That made eight states. The next one would do the trick.

In New Hampshire, in June, the convention was sitting again, this time at Portsmouth. It would be close. Those who lived along the state's skimpy seaboard as well as those who lived along the Connecticut River were for the Constitution, but the inland farmers were dead set against it.

At the same time the momentous Virginia convention was under way at Richmond. This was a slam-bang affair, with George Mason and the inexorably homespun, determinedly uncouth Patrick Henry pulling out all the oratorical stops on the anti side—Henry spoke all day at one session—while the unimpressive but deadly earnest James Madison and handsome Edmund Randolph (who had at last decided that he should support the Constitution) plugged away for the pros. At one time so heated were the words that friends of Patrick Henry, the former governor, and of Edmund Randolph, the current governor, were conferring quietly out of doors. It would have been an interesting confrontation between those two, and the document from Philadelphia might have won its first martyr. However, it was settled without pistols.

The end came June 25, after a torrid three weeks of

We the People

Article I

THE CONSTITUTION OF THE UNITED STATES

speeches. The Constitution won, 89 to 79. There was jubilation, for the Federalists supposed that this made Virginia the ninth and clinching state. In fact, as they were soon to learn, New Hampshire had ratified four days earlier, 57 to 46.

That made ten, one more than was needed. North Carolina, for reasons not clear to the others, and perhaps not overly patent to the North Carolinians themselves, was being balky. Cantankerous little Rhode Island, of course, never could be counted upon.

But New York . . .

Geographically, in this connection, New York was the most important state of them all. It was wedged down between New England on the east and the rest of the country on the south, and without it the new republic would be hopelessly split, probably unmanageable.

George Clinton had been governor for eleven years and he looked unbeatable. The convention was held at Poughkeepsie, starting June 17. Alexander Hamilton, leading the Federalist forces, played every trick at his command in order to postpone a final vote, it being his conviction that if New Hampshire and Virginia fell into line New York would be obliged to do so too. He had posted riders at both of those conventions, at his own expense. Meanwhile he spoke, and spoke. His principal opponent—Yates and Lansing were not very effective in debate—was Melancton Smith, a self-made merchant from New York City. The thing dragged on for weeks, the longest of the conventions.

Out of doors the Federalists were being more forceful.

The pattern was repeated. The commercial classes, crowded into the southeast corner of the state, comprising New York City and its environs, were strong for the Constitution; the upstate farmers were opposed. Now Clinton and his men were being told, bluntly—though it was never committed to paper—that unless they got into the Union this vital small triangle, controlling the mouth of the Hudson, would declare itself free and independent.

It might have been a bluff, but it rocked the Clintonians.

Upstate, though so much bigger, could not possibly have subsisted without the city of New York.

On June 24, the news came from New Hampshire. That didn't rock anybody. New Hampshire was small and far away.

On July 2, the news came from Virginia. That was something else again.

Still they hammered away at one another, the Hamilton forces, the Federalists, gaining strength all the time, until at last Melancton Smith publicly and frankly declared himself beaten. He had been convinced. He would vote for the Constitution, which in fact won, July 26, by a vote of 30 to 27.

Like Massachusetts, like Virginia, New York did submit to the yet-to-be-born Congress a list of bill-of-rights items which she thought should be added to the Constitution, but like the others again she did not make acceptance of this list a *sine qua non* for ratification. It was only a suggestion. Here, then, was a clear-cut victory for the Federalists.

There were about 3,000,000 persons in the country at the time, and about 150,000 of them voted in the various ratification conventions, two-thirds for the Constitution.

North Carolina was not to come in until the end of the following year, Rhode Island not until May of 1790.

Meanwhile, on July 2, 1788, the Continental Congress (thereby signing its own death warrant) notified the world that the United States had a Constitution.

Notes

1. James Bowdoin, father of the James Bowdoin who founded Bowdoin College in Maine. Maine at that time still was a part of Massachusetts.

2. It was customary in the British Army of that time—and the custom was carried over into the American Army—to count forces by rank and file, which included all privates, noncommissioned officers, musicians, etc., though not chaplains or surgeons. The percentage of rank and file to officers varied, but it was generally between 12 and 15 to 1.

3. The word "dollar" came from the Spanish, but its most distant origin is German, it being a corruption of "thaler," which in turn derives from Joachimstaler or the silver of Joachimstahl, Bohemia, where, in the sixteenth century, most of it did come from. The Spanish dollar was a silver coin about the size of the present U.S. silver dollar, and it was worth eight Spanish reals. For this reason they were often called eight-pieces, or, as Long John Silver's parrot put it, "pieces of eight."

4. Today we call it lobbying.

5. It was he who, fourteen years later, was to sell to Eleuthère Irénée du Pont de Nemours his farm of ninety-five acres on the Brandywine, the germ out of which grew the Du Pont empire.

6. A famous fort was to be named after him, the one that defended Baltimore against British attack in the War of 1812, inspiring Francis Scott Key to write: "Oh, say can you see . . ."

7. The official journal of the convention was not printed until the year 1816. It is very dull.

8. He was the hero—or at any rate the principal male character—in Mary Anne, Daphne du Maurier's novel based on that scandal.

9. The city of Paterson, New Jersey, was to be named after him a few years later.

Appendix

THE VIRGINIA PLAN

1. Resolved, That the articles of Confederation ought to be so corrected and enlarged as to accomplish the objects proposed by their institution; namely, common defence, security of liberty and general welfare.

2. Resolved, therefore, That the rights of suffrage in the National Legislature ought to be proportioned to the Quotas of contribution, or to the number of free inhabitants, as the one or the other rule may seem best in different cases.

3. Resolved, That the National Legislature ought to consist of two branches.

4. Resolved, That the members of the first branch of the National Legislature ought to be elected by the people of the several States every   for the term of   ; to be of the age of   years at least; to receive liberal stipends by which they may be compensated for the devotion of their time to public service; to be ineligible to any office established by a particular State, or under the authority of the United States, except those peculiarly belonging to the functions of the first branch, during the term of service, and for the space of   after its expiration; to be incapable of re-election for the space of   after the expiration of their term of service; and to be subject to recall.

5. Resolved, That the members of the second branch of the National Legislature ought to be elected by those of the first, out of a proper number of persons nominated by the individual Legislatures; to be of the age of   years, at least; to hold their offices for a term sufficient to ensure their independency;

169

to receive liberal stipends, by which they may be compensated for the devotion of their time to public service; and to be ineligible to any office established by a particular State, or under the authority of the United States, except those peculiarly belonging to the functions of the second branch, during the term of service, and for the space of   after the expiration thereof.

6. Resolved, That each branch ought to possess the right of originating Acts; that the National Legislature ought to be impowered to enjoy the Legislative rights vested in Congress by the Confederation, and moreover to legislate in all cases to which the separate States are incompetent, or in which the harmony of the United States may be interrupted by the exercise of individual Legislation; to negative all laws passed by the several States, contravening in the opinion of the National Legislature the articles of Union; and to call forth the forces of the Union against any member of the Union failing to fulfill its duty under the articles thereof.

7. Resolved, That a national executive be instituted; to be chosen by the National Legislature for a term of   years; to receive punctually at stated times a fixed compensation for the services rendered, in which no increase or diminution shall be made so as to affect the Magistracy existing at the time of increase or diminution; and to be ineligible a second time; and that besides a general authority to execute the National laws, it ought to enjoy the Executive rights vested in Congress by the Confederation.

8. Resolved, That the executive and a convenient number of the National Judiciary, ought to compose a council of revision with authority to examine every act of the National Legislature before it shall operate, and every act of a particular Legislature before a Negative thereon shall be final; and that the dissent of the said Council shall amount to be rejection, unless the act of the National Legislature be again passed, or that of a particular Legislature be again negatived by   of the members of each branch.

9. Resolved, That a national judiciary be established to

consist of one or more supreme tribunals, and of inferior tribunals to be chosen by the National Legislature, to hold their offices during good behavior; and to receive punctually at stated times fixed compensations for their services, in which no increase or diminution shall be made so as to affect the person actually in office at the time of such increase or diminution. That the jurisdiction of the inferior tribunals shall be to hear and determine in the first instance, and of the supreme tribunal to hear and determine, in the dernier resort, all piracies and felonies on the high seas; captures from an enemy; cases in which foreigners or citizens of other States applying to such jurisdictions may be interested, or which respect the collection of the National revenue; impeachments of any National officer; and questions which involve the national peace or harmony.

10. Resolved, That provision ought to be made for the admission of States lawfully arising within the limits of the United States, whether from a voluntary junction of Government and Territory, or otherwise, with the consent of a number of voices in the National Legislature less than the whole.

11. Resolved, That a Republican Government and the territory of each State, except in the instance of a voluntary junction of Government and territory, ought to be guaranteed by the United States to each State.

12. Resolved, That provision ought to be made for the continuance of Congress and their authorities and privileges, until a given day after the reform of the articles of Union shall be adopted, and for the completion of all their engagements.

13. Resolved, That provision ought to be made for the amendment of the articles of Union whensoever it shall seem necessary; and that the assent of the National Legislature ought not to be required thereto.

14. Resolved, That the legislative, executive, and judiciary powers within the several States ought to be bound by oath to support the articles of union.

15. Resolved, That the amendments which shall be offered to the Confederation, by the Convention ought at a proper time, or times, after the approbation of Congress, to be sub-

mitted to an assembly or assemblies of Representatives, recommended by the several Legislatures to be expressly chosen by the people, to consider and decide thereon.

THE NEW JERSEY PLAN

1. Resolved, That the articles of Confederation ought to be so revised, corrected and enlarged, as to render the federal Constitution adequate to the exigencies of Government, and the preservation of the Union.

2. Resolved, That in addition to the powers vested in the United States in Congress, by the present existing articles of Confederation, they be authorized to pass acts for raising a revenue, by levying a duty or duties on all goods and merchandizes of foreign growth or manufacture, imported into any part of the United States, by Stamps on paper, vellum or parchment, and by a postage on all letters and packages passing through the general post-office, to be applied to such federal purposes as they shall deem proper and expedient; to make rules and regulations for the collection thereof; and the same from time to time, to alter and amend in such manner as they shall think proper; to pass Acts for the regulation of trade and commerce, as well with foreign nations as with each other: provided that all punishments, fines, forfeitures, and penalties to be incurred for contravening such rules and regulations shall be adjudged by the Common law Judiciaries of the State in which any offence contrary to the true intent and meaning of such Acts, rules and regulations shall have been committed or perpetrated, with liberty of commencing in the first instance all suits or prosecutions for that purpose, in the superior Common law Judiciary of such State; subject nevertheless, for the correction of errors, both in law and fact in rendering judgment, to an appeal to the Judiciary of the United States.

3. Resolved, That whenever requisitions shall be necessary, instead of the rule for making requisitions mentioned in the articles of Confederation the United States in Congress be

authorized to make such requisitions in proportion to the whole number of white and other free citizens and inhabitants of every age, sex, and condition, including those bound to servitude for a term of years, and three fifths of all other persons not comprehended in the foregoing description, except Indians not paying taxes; that if such requisitions be not complied with, in the time specified therein, to direct the collection thereof in the non-complying States, and for that purpose to devise and pass acts directing and authorizing the same; provided that none of the powers hereby vested in the United States in Congress shall be exercised without the consent of at least   States; and in that proportion, if the number of confederated States should hereafter be increased or diminished.

4. Resolved, That the United States in Congress be authorized to elect a federal Executive to consist of   persons, to continue in office for the term of   years; to receive punctually at stated times a fixed compensation for their services in which no increase or diminution shall be made so as to affect the persons composing the Executive at the time of such increase or diminution, to be paid out of the federal treasury; to be incapable of holding any other office or appointment during their term of service, and for   years thereafter: to be ineligible a second time, and removable by Congress on application by a majority of the Executives of the several States; that the executive, besides their general authority to execute the federal acts ought to appoint all federal officers not otherwise provided for, and to direct all military operations; provided, that none of the persons composing the Federal Executive shall, on any occasion, take command of any troops, so as personally to conduct any military enterprise as General, or in any other capacity.

5. Resolved, That a federal Judiciary be established, to consist of a supreme Tribune the Judges of which to be appointed by the Executive, and to hold their offices during good behavior; to receive punctually at stated times a fixed compensation for their services, in which no increase or diminution shall be made, so as to affect the persons actually in office at the

time of such increase or diminution. That the Judiciary so established shall have authority to hear and determine in the first instance on all impeachments of federal officers, and by way of appeal in the dernier resort in all cases touching the rights and privileges of Ambassadors; in all cases of captures from an enemy; in all cases of piracies and felonies on the high seas; in all cases in which foreigners may be interested, in the construction of any treaty or treaties, or which may arise on any of the acts for regulation of trade, or the collection of the federal Revenue. That none of the Judiciary shall during the time they remain in Office be capable of receiving or holding any other office or appointment during their term of service, or for thereafter.

6. Resolved, That all acts of the United States in Congress, made by virtue and in pursuance of the powers hereby and by the articles of confederation vested in them, and all treaties made and ratified under the authority of the United States, shall be the supreme law of the respective States as far forth as those Acts or Treaties shall relate to the said States or their Citizens; and that the judiciary of the several States shall be bound thereby in their decisions, any thing in the respective laws of the Individual States to the contrary notwithstanding; and if any State, or any body of men in any State, shall oppose or prevent the carrying into execution such acts or treaties, the federal Executive shall be authorized to call forth the powers of the Confederated States, or so much thereof as may be necessary, to enforce and compel an obedience to such Acts, or an Observance of such Treaties.

7. Resolved, That provision be made for the admission of new States into the Union.

8. Resolved, That the rule for naturalization ought to be the same in every State.

9. Resolved, That a citizen of one State committing an offence in another State of the Union shall be deemed guilty of the same offence as if it had been committed by a citizen of the State in which the offence was committed.

CONSTITUTION OF THE UNITED STATES

PREAMBLE

We, the People of the United States, in Order to form a more perfect Union, establish Justice, insure domestic Tranquility, provide for the common defence, promote the general Welfare, and secure the Blessings of Liberty to ourselves and our Posterity, do ordain and establish this Constitution for the United States of America.

ARTICLE I

Section 1. All legislative Powers herein granted shall be vested in a Congress of the United States, which shall consist of a Senate and House of Representatives.

Section 2. The House of Representatives shall be composed of Members chosen every second Year by the People of the several States, and the Electors in each State shall have the Qualifications requisite for Electors of the most numerous Branch of the State Legislature.

No Person shall be a Representative who shall not have attained to the Age of twenty-five Years, and been seven Years a Citizen of the United States, and who shall not, when elected, be an Inhabitant of that State in which he shall be chosen.

Representatives and direct Taxes shall be apportioned among the several States which may be included within this Union, according to their respective Numbers, which shall be determined by adding to the whole Number of free Persons, including those bound to Service for a Term of Years, and excluding Indians not taxed, three-fifths of all other Persons. The actual Enumeration shall be made within three Years after the first Meeting of the Congress of the United States, and within every subsequent Term of ten Years, in such Manner as they shall by Law direct. The Number of Representatives shall not exceed one for every thirty Thousand, but each State shall have at Least one Representative; and until such enumeration shall be made, the State of New Hampshire shall be entitled to choose three, Massachusetts eight, Rhode-Island and Providence Plantations one, Connecticut five, New-York six, New Jersey four, Pennsylvania eight, Delaware one, Maryland six, Virginia ten, North Carolina five, South Carolina five, and Georgia three.

When vacancies happen in the Representation from any State, the Executive Authority thereof shall issue Writs of Election to fill such Vacancies.

The House of Representatives shall choose their Speaker and other Officers; and shall have the sole Power of Impeachment.

Section 3. The Senate of the United States shall be composed of two Senators from each State, chosen by the Legislature thereof, for six Years; and each Senator shall have one Vote.

Immediately after they shall be assembled in Consequence of the first Election, they shall be divided as equally as may be into three Classes. The Seats of the Senators of the first Class shall be vacated at the Expiration of the second Year, of the second Class at the Expiration of the fourth Year, and of the third Class at the Expiration of the sixth Year, so that one-third may be chosen every second Year; and if Vacancies happen by Resignation, or otherwise, during the Recess of the Legislature of any State, the Executive thereof may make temporary Appointment until the next Meeting of the Legislature, which shall then fill such Vacancies.

No Person shall be a Senator who shall not have attained to the Age of thirty Years, and been nine Years a Citizen of the United States, and who shall not, when elected, be an Inhabitant of that State for which he shall be chosen.

The Vice-President of the United States shall be President of the Senate, but shall have no vote, unless they be equally divided.

The Senate shall choose their other Officers, and also a President pro tempore, in the Absence of the Vice-President, or when he shall exercise the Office of President of the United States.

The Senate shall have the sole Power to try all Impeachments. When sitting for that Purpose, they shall be on Oath or Affirmation. When the President of the United States is tried, the Chief Justice shall preside: And no Person shall be convicted without the Concurrence of two-thirds of the Members present.

Judgment of Cases of Impeachment shall not extend further than to removal from Office, and disqualification to hold and enjoy any office of honor, Trust or Profit under the United States: but the Party convicted shall nevertheless be liable and subject to Indictment, Trial, Judgment and Punishment, according to Law.

Section 4. The Times, Places and Manner of holding Elec tions for Senators and Representatives shall be prescribed ir each State by the Legislature thereof; but the Congress may a any time by Law make or alter such Regulations, except as t the Places of choosing Senators.

The Congress shall assemble at least once in every Yea and such Meeting shall be on the first Monday in Decembe unless they shall by Law appoint a different Day.

Section 5. Each House shall be the Judge of the Electio Returns and Qualifications of its own Members, and a Major of each shall constitute a Quorum to do Business, but a sma Number may adjourn from day to day, and may be authori to compel the Attendance of absent Members, in such Man and under such Penalties as each House may provide.

Each House may determine the Rules of its Proceed punish its Members for disorderly Behaviour, and, with Concurrence of two-thirds, expel a Member.

Each House shall keep a Journal of its Proceedings from time to time publish the same, excepting such Pa may in their Judgment require Secrecy; and the Yeas and of the Members of either House on any question shall, Desire of one-fifth of those Present, be entered on the Jo

Neither House, during the Session of Congress, shall, without the Consent of the other, adjourn for more than three days, nor to any other Place than that in which the two Houses shall be sitting.

Section 6. The Senators and Representatives shall receive a Compensation for their Services, to be ascertained by Law, and paid out of the Treasury of the United States. They shall in all Cases, except Treason, Felony and Breach of the Peace, be privileged from Arrest during their Attendance at the Session of their respective Houses, and in going to and returning from the same; and for any Speech or Debate in either House, they shall not be questioned in any other Place.

No Senator or Representative shall, during the Time for which he was elected, be appointed to any civil Office under the Authority of the United States, which shall have been created, or the Emoluments whereof shall have been increased during such time; and no Person holding any Office under the United States, shall be a Member of either House during his Continuance in Office.

Section 7. All Bills for raising Revenue shall originate in the House of Representatives; but the Senate may propose or concur with Amendments as on other Bills.

Every Bill which shall have passed the House of Representatives and the Senate shall, before it becomes a Law, be presented to the President of the United States; If he approve, he shall sign it, but if not, he shall return it, with his Objections, to that House in which it shall have originated, who shall enter the Objections at large on their Journal, and proceed to reconsider it. If after such Reconsideration two-thirds of the House shall agree to pass the Bill, it shall be sent, together with the Objections, to the other House, by which it shall likewise be reconsidered, and if approved by two-thirds of that House, it shall become a Law. But in all such Cases the Votes of both Houses shall be determined by Yeas and Nays, and the Names of the Persons voting for and against the Bill shall be entered on the Journal of each House respectively. If any Bill shall not be returned by the President within ten Days (Sundays excepted)

after it shall have been presented to him, the Same shall be a Law, in like Manner as if he had signed it, unless the Congress by their Adjournment prevent its Return, in which Case it shall not be a Law.

Every Order, Resolution, or Vote to which the Concurrence of the Senate and House of Representatives may be necessary (except on a question of Adjournment) shall be presented to the President of the United States; and before the Same shall take Effect, shall be approved by him, or being disapproved by him, shall be repassed by two-thirds of the Senate and House of Representatives, according to the Rules and Limitations prescribed in the Case of a Bill.

Section 8. The Congress shall have Power: To lay and collect Taxes, Duties, Imposts and Excises, to pay the Debts and provide for the common Defence and general Welfare of the United States; but all Duties, Imposts and Excises shall be uniform throughout the United States;

To borrow Money on the credit of the United States;

To regulate Commerce with foreign Nations, and among the several States, and with the Indian Tribes;

To establish an uniform Rule of Naturalization, and uniform Laws on the subject of Bankruptcies throughout the United States;

To coin Money, regulate the Value thereof, and of foreign Coin, and fix the Standard of Weights and Measures;

To provide for the Punishment of counterfeiting the Securities and current Coin of the United States;

To establish Post Offices and post Roads;

To promote the Progress of Science and useful Arts, by securing for limited Times to Authors and Inventors the exclusive Right to their respective Writings and Discoveries;

To constitute Tribunals inferior to the supreme Court;

To define and punish Piracies and Felonies committed on the high Seas, and Offences against the Law of Nations;

To declare War, grant Letters of Marque and Reprisal, and make Rules concerning captures on Land and Water;

To raise and support Armies, but no Appropriation of

Money to that Use shall be for a longer Term than two Years;

To provide and maintain a Navy;

To make Rules for the Government and Regulation of the land and naval Forces;

To provide for calling forth the Militia to execute the Laws of the Union, suppress Insurrections and repel Invasions;

To provide for organizing, arming, and disciplining the Militia, and for governing such Part of them as may be employed in the Service of the United States, reserving to the States respectively, the Appointment of the Officers, and the Authority of training the Militia according to the discipline prescribed by Congress;

To exercise exclusive Legislation in all Cases whatsoever, over such District (not exceeding ten Miles square) as may be, by Cession of particular States, and the Acceptance of Congress, become the Seat of Government of the United States, and to exercise like Authority over all Places purchased by the Consent of the Legislature of the State in which the Same shall be, for the Erection of Forts, Magazines, Arsenals, dock-Yards, and other needful Buildings;—And

To make all Laws which shall be necessary and proper for carrying into Execution the foregoing Powers, and all other Powers vested by this Constitution in the Government of the United States, or in any Department or Officer thereof.

Section 9. The Migration or Importation of such Persons as any of the States now existing shall think proper to admit, shall not be prohibited by the Congress prior to the Year one thousand eight hundred and eight, but a Tax or duty may be imposed on such Importation, not exceeding ten dollars for each Person.

The Privilege of the Writ of Habeas Corpus shall not be suspended, unless when in Cases of Rebellion or Invasion the public Safety may require it.

No Bill of Attainder or ex post facto Law shall be passed.

No Capitation, or other direct, Tax shall be laid unless in Proportion to the Census or Enumeration herein before directed to be taken.

No tax or Duty shall be laid on Articles exported from any State.

No Preference shall be given by any Regulation of Commerce or Revenue to the Ports of one State over those of another: nor shall Vessels bound to, or from, one State, be obliged to enter, clear, or pay Duties in another.

No Money shall be drawn from the Treasury, but in Consequence of Appropriations made by Law; and a regular Statement and Account of the Receipts and Expenditures of all public Money shall be published from time to time.

No Title of Nobility shall be granted by the United States; And no Person holding any Office of Profit or Trust under them, shall, without the Consent of the Congress, accept of any present, Emolument, Office, or Title, of any kind whatever, from any King, Prince, or foreign State.

Section 10. No State shall enter into any Treaty, Alliance, or Confederation; grant Letters of Marque and Reprisal; coin Money; emit Bills of Credit; make any Thing but gold and silver Coin a Tender in Payment of Debts; pass any Bill of Attainder, ex post facto Law, or Law impairing the Obligation of Contracts, or grant any Title of Nobility.

No State shall, without the Consent of the Congress, lay any Imposts or Duties on Imports or Exports, except what may be absolutely necessary for executing its inspection Laws: and the net Produce of all Duties and Imposts, laid by any State on Imports or Exports, shall be for the Use of the Treasury of the United States; and all such Laws shall be subject to the Revision and Control of the Congress.

No State shall, without the Consent of Congress, lay any Duty of Tonnage, keep Troops, or Ships of War in time of Peace, enter into any Agreement or Compact with another State, or with a foreign Power, or engage in War, unless actually invaded, or in such imminent Danger as will not admit of delay.

ARTICLE II

Section 1. The executive Power shall be vested in a President of the United States of America. He shall hold his Office during the Term of four Years, and, together with the Vice-President, chosen for the same Term, be elected, as follows:

Each State shall appoint, in such Manner as the Legislature thereof may direct, a Number of Electors, equal to the whole Number of Senators and Representatives to which the State may be entitled in the Congress: but no Senator or Representative, or Person holding an Office of Trust or Profit under the United States, shall be appointed an Elector.

The Electors shall meet in their respective States, and vote by Ballot for two Persons, of whom one at least shall not be an inhabitant of the same State with themselves. And they shall make a List of all the Persons voted for, and of the Number of Votes for each; which List they shall sign and certify, and transmit sealed to the Seat of the Government of the United States, directed to the President of the Senate. The President of the Senate shall, in the Presence of the Senate and House of Representatives, open all the Certificates, and the Votes shall then be counted. The Person having the greatest Number of Votes shall be the President, if such Number be a Majority of the whole Number of Electors appointed; and if there be more than one who have such Majority, and have an equal Number of Votes, then the House of Representatives shall immediately choose by Ballot one of them for President; and if no Person have a majority, then from the five highest on the List the said House shall in like Manner choose the President. But in choosing the President, the Votes shall be taken by States, the Representation from each State having one Vote. A quorum for this Purpose shall consist of a Member or Members from two-thirds of the States, and a Majority of all the States shall be necessary to a Choice. In every Case, after the Choice of the President, the Person having the greatest Number of Votes of the Electors shall be the Vice-President. But if there should remain two or more who have equal Votes, the Senate shall choose from them by Ballot the Vice-President.

The Congress may determine the Time of choosing the Electors, and the Day on which they shall give their Votes; which Day shall be the same throughout the United States.

No Person except a natural born Citizen, or a Citizen of the United States, at the time of the Adoption of this Constitution, shall be eligible to that Office who shall not have attained to the Age of thirty-five Years, and been fourteen Years a Resident within the United States.

In Case of the Removal of the President from Office, or of his Death, Resignation, or Inability to discharge the Powers and Duties of the said Office, the Same shall devolve on the Vice-President, and the Congress may by Law provide for the Case of Removal, Death, Resignation or Inability, both of the President and Vice-President, declaring what Officer shall then act as President, and such Officer shall act accordingly, until the Disability be removed, or a President shall be elected.

The President shall, at stated times, receive for his services, a Compensation, which shall neither be increased nor diminished during the Period for which he shall have been elected, and he shall not receive within that Period any other Emolument from the United States, or any of them.

Before he enter on the Execution of his Office, he shall take the following Oath or Affirmation:—"I do solemnly swear (or affirm) that I will faithfully execute the office of President of the United States, and will, to the best of my Ability, preserve, protect and defend the Constitution of the United States."

Section 2. The President shall be Commander-in-Chief of the Army and Navy of the United States, and of the Militia of the several States, when called into the actual Service of the United States; he may require the Opinion, in writing, of the principal Officer in each of the executive Departments, upon any Subject relating to the Duties of their respective Offices, and he shall have Power to grant Reprieves and Pardons for all

Offences against the United States, except in Cases of Impeachment.

He shall have Power, by and with the Advice and Consent of the Senate, to make Treaties, provided two-thirds of the Senators present concur; and he shall nominate, and by and with the Advice and Consent of the Senate, shall appoint Ambassadors, other public Ministers and Consuls, Judges of the Supreme Court, and all other Officers of the United States, whose Appointments are not herein otherwise provided for, and which shall be established by Law: but the Congress may by Law vest the Appointment of such inferior Officers, as they think proper, in the President alone, in the Courts of Law, or in the Heads of Departments.

The President shall have power to fill up all vacancies that may happen during the Recess of the Senate, by granting Commissions which shall expire at the End of their next Session.

Section 3. He shall from time to time give to the Congress Information of the State of the Union, and recommend to their Consideration such Measures as he shall judge necessary and expedient; he may, on extraordinary Occasions, convene both Houses, or either of them, and in Case of Disagreement between them, with Respect to the Time of Adjournment, he may adjourn them to such Time as he shall think proper; he shall receive Ambassadors and other public Ministers; he shall take Care that the Laws be faithfully executed, and shall Commission all the Officers of the United States.

Section 4. The President, Vice-President and all civil Officers of the United States, shall be removed from Office on Impeachment for, and Conviction of, Treason, Bribery, or other High Crimes and Misdemeanors.

ARTICLE III

Section 1. The judicial Power of the United States shall be vested in one Supreme Court, and in such inferior Courts as the Congress may from time to time ordain and establish. The Judges, both of the Supreme and inferior Courts, shall hold their Offices during good Behaviour, and shall, at stated Times, receive for their Services, a Compensation, which shall not be diminished during their Continuance in Office.

Section 2. The judicial Power shall extend to all Cases, in Law and Equity, arising under this Constitution, the Laws of the United States, and Treaties made, or which shall be made, under their Authority;—to all Cases affecting Ambassadors, other public Ministers and Consuls;—to all Cases of admiralty and maritime Jurisdiction;—to Controversies to which the United States shall be a Party;—to Controversies between two or more States;—between a State and Citizens of another State; —between Citizens of different States;—between Citizens of the same State claiming Lands under Grants of different States, and between a State, or the Citizens thereof, and foreign States, Citizens or Subjects.

In all Cases affecting Ambassadors, other public Ministers and Consuls, and those in which a State shall be Party, the Supreme Court shall have original Jurisdiction. In all the other Cases before mentioned, the Supreme Court shall have appellate Jurisdiction, both as to Law and Fact, with such Exceptions, and under such Regulations as the Congress shall make.

The Trial of all Crimes, except in Cases of Impeachment, shall be by Jury; and such Trial shall be held in the State where the said Crimes shall have been committed; but when not committed within any State, the Trial shall be at such Place or Places as the Congress may by Law have directed.

Section 3. Treason against the United States, shall consist only in levying War against them, or in adhering to their Enemies, giving them Aid and Comfort. No Person shall be convicted of Treason unless on the Testimony of two Witnesses to the same overt Act, or on Confession in open Court.

The Congress shall have Power to declare the Punishment of Treason, but no Attainder of Treason shall work Corruption of Blood, or Forfeiture except during the Life of the Person attainted.

ARTICLE IV

Section 1. Full Faith and Credit shall be given in each State to the public Acts, Records and judicial Proceedings of every other State. And the Congress may by general Laws prescribe the Manner in which such Acts, Records and Proceedings shall be proved, and the Effect thereof.

Section 2. The Citizens of each State shall be entitled to all Privileges and Immunities of Citizens in the several States.

A Person charged in any State with Treason, Felony, or other Crime, who shall flee from Justice, and be found in another State, shall on Demand of the executive Authority of the State from which he fled, be delivered up, to be removed to the State having Jurisdiction of the Crime.

No Person held to Service or Labour in one State, under the Laws thereof, escaping into another, shall, in Consequence of any Law or Regulation therein, be discharged from such Service or Labour, but shall be delivered up on Claim of the Party to whom such Service or Labour may be due.

Section 3. New States may be admitted by the Congress into this Union; but no new State shall be formed or erected within the Jurisdiction of any other State; nor any State be formed by the Junction of two or more States, or Parts of States, without the Consent of the Legislatures of the States concerned as well as of the Congress.

The Congress shall have Power to dispose of and make all needful Rules and Regulations respecting the Territory or other Property belonging to the United States; and nothing in this Constitution shall be so construed as to Prejudice any Claims of the United States, or of any particular State.

Section 4. The United States shall guarantee to every State in this Union a Republican Form of Government, and shall protect each of them against Invasion; and on Application of the Legislature, or of the Executive (when the Legislature cannot be convened) against domestic Violence.

ARTICLE V

The Congress, whenever two-thirds of both Houses shall deem it necessary, shall propose Amendments to this Constitution, or, on the Application of the Legislatures of two-thirds of the several States, shall call a Convention for proposing Amendments, which, in either Case, shall be valid to all Intents and Purposes, as Part of this Constitution, when ratified by the Legislatures of three-fourths of the several States, or by Conventions in three-fourths thereof, as the one or the other Mode of Ratification may be proposed by the Congress; Provided that no Amendment which may be made prior to the Year One thousand eight hundred and eight shall in any Manner affect the first and fourth Clauses in the Ninth Section of the first Article; and that no State, without its Consent, shall be deprived of its equal Suffrage in the Senate.

ARTICLE VI

All Debts contracted and Engagements entered into, before the Adoption of this Constitution, shall be as valid against the United States under this Constitution as under the Confederation.

This Constitution, and the Laws of the United States which shall be made in Pursuance thereof and all Treaties made, or which shall be made, under the Authority of the United States, shall be the supreme Law of the Land; and the Judges in every State shall be bound thereby, any Thing in the Constitution or Laws of any State to the Contrary notwithstanding.

The Senators and Representatives before mentioned, and the Members of the several State Legislatures, and all executive and judicial Officers, both of the United States and of the Several States, shall be bound by Oath or Affirmation, to support this Constitution; but no religious Test shall ever be required as a Qualification to any Office or public Trust under the United States.

ARTICLE VII

The ratification of the Conventions of nine States, shall be sufficient for the Establishment of this Constitution between the States so ratifying the Same.

Done in Convention by the Unanimous Consent of the States present the Seventeenth Day of September in the Year of our Lord one thousand seven hundred and Eighty-seven, and of the Independence of the United States of America the Twelfth. In witness whereof We have hereunto subscribed our Names, Attest

William Jackson
Secretary

Go: Washington—
Presidt. and deputy from Virginia

NEW HAMPSHIRE
John Langdon
Nicholas Gilman

MASSACHUSETTS
Nathaniel Gorham
Rufus King

CONNECTICUT
Wm. Saml. Johnson
Roger Sherman

NEW YORK
Alexander Hamilton

NEW JERSEY
Wil: Livingston
David Brearley
William Paterson
Jona: Dayton

PENNSYLVANIA
B. Franklin
Thomas Mifflin
Robt. Morris
Geo. Clymer
Thos. Fitzsimons
Jared Ingersoll
James Wilson
Gouv Morris

DELAWARE
Geo: Read
Gunning Bedford Jun
John Dickinson
Richard Bassett
Jaco: Broom

MARYLAND
James McHenry
Dan of St. Thos Jenifer
Danl. Carroll

VIRGINIA
John Blair—
James Madison, Jr.

NORTH CAROLINA
William Blount
Richd. Dobbs Spaight
Hu Williamson

SOUTH CAROLINA
J. Rutledge
Charles Cotesworth Pinckney
Charles Pinckney
Pierce Butler

GEORGIA
William Few
Abr Baldwin

AMENDMENTS

ARTICLE I

Congress shall make no law respecting an establishment of religion, or prohibiting the free exercise thereof; or abridging the freedom of speech, or of the press; or the right of the people peaceably to assemble, and to petition the Government for a redress of grievances.

ARTICLE II

A well-regulated Militia, being necessary to the security of a free State, the right of the people to keep and bear Arms, shall not be infringed.

ARTICLE III

No Soldier shall, in time of peace be quartered in any house, without the consent of the Owner, nor in time of war, but in a manner to be prescribed by law.

Article IV

The right of the people to be secure in their persons, houses, papers, and effects against unreasonable searches and seizures, shall not be violated, and no Warrants shall issue, but upon probable cause, supported by Oath or affirmation, and particularly describing the place to be searched, and the persons or things to be seized.

Article V

No person shall be held to answer for a capital, or other infamous crime, unless on a presentment or indictment of a Grand Jury, except in cases arising in the land or naval forces, or in the Militia, when in actual service in time of War or public danger; nor shall any person be subject for the same offence to be twice put in jeopardy of life or limb; nor shall be compelled in any criminal case to be a witness against himself, nor be deprived of life, liberty, or property, without due process of law, nor shall private property be taken for public use, without just compensation.

Article VI

In all criminal prosecutions, the accused shall enjoy the right to a speedy and public trial, by an impartial jury of the State and district wherein the crime shall have been committed, which district shall have been previously ascertained by law, and to be informed of the nature and cause of the accusation; to be confronted with the witnesses against him; to have compulsory process for obtaining witnesses in his favor, and to have the Assistance of Counsel for his defence.

Article VII

In Suits at common law, where the value in controversy shall exceed twenty dollars, the right of trial by jury shall be preserved, and no fact tried by a jury, shall be otherwise re-examined in any Court of the United States, than according to the rules of the common law.

Article VIII

Excessive bail shall not be required, nor excessive fines imposed, nor cruel and unusual punishments inflicted.

Article IX

The enumeration in the Constitution, of certain rights, shall not be construed to deny or disparage others retained by the people.

Article X

The powers not delegated to the United States by the Constitution, nor prohibited by it to the States, are reserved to the States respectively, or to the people.

Article XI

The Judicial power of the United States shall not be construed to extend to any suit in law or equity, commenced or prosecuted against one of the United States by Citizens of another State, or by Citizens or Subjects of any Foreign State.

Article XII

The Electors shall meet in their respective states, and vote by ballot for President and Vice-President, one of whom, at least, shall not be an inhabitant of the same state with themselves; they shall name in their ballots the person voted for as President, and in distinct ballots the person voted for as President, and of all persons voted for as Vice-President, and of the number of votes for each, which lists they shall sign and certify, and transmit sealed to the seat of the government of the United States, directed to the President of the Senate;—The President of the Senate shall, in the presence of the Senate and House of Representatives, open all the certificates and the votes shall then be counted;—the person having the greatest number of votes for President, shall be the President, if such number be a majority of the whole number of Electors appointed; and if no person have such majority, then from the persons having the highest numbers not exceeding three on the list of those voted for as President, the House of Representatives shall choose immediately, by ballot, the President. But in choosing the President, the votes shall be taken by states, the representation from each state having one vote; a quorum for this purpose shall consist of a member or members from two-thirds of the states, and a majority of all the states shall be necessary to a choice. And if the House of Representatives shall not choose a President whenever the right of choice shall devolve upon them, before the fourth day of March next following, then the Vice-President shall act as President, as in the case of the death or other constitutional disability of the President.—The person having the greatest number of votes as Vice-President, shall be the Vice-President, if such number be a majority of the whole number of Electors appointed, and if no person have a majority, then from the two highest numbers on the list, the Senate shall choose the Vice-President; a quorum for the purpose shall consist of two-thirds of the whole number of Senators, and a majority of the whole number shall be necessary to a choice. But no person constitutionally ineligible to the office of President shall be eligible to that of Vice-President of the United States.

ARTICLE XIII

Section 1. Neither slavery nor involuntary servitude, except as a punishment for crime whereof the party shall have been duly convicted, shall exist within the United States, or any place subject to their jurisdiction.

Section 2. Congress shall have power to enforce this article by appropriate legislation.

ARTICLE XIV

Section 1. All persons born or naturalized in the United States, and subject to the jurisdiction thereof, are citizens of the United States and of the State wherein they reside. No State shall make or enforce any law which shall abridge the privileges or immunities of citizens of the United States; nor shall any

State deprive any person of life, liberty, or property, without due process of law; nor deny to any person within its jurisdiction the equal protection of the laws.

Section. 2. Representatives shall be apportioned among the several States according to their respective numbers, counting the whole number of persons in each State, excluding Indians not taxed. But when the right to vote at any election for the choice of electors for President and Vice-President of the United States, Representatives in Congress, and Executive and Judicial officers of a State, or the members of the Legislature thereof, is denied to any of the male members of such State, being twenty-one years of age, and citizens of the United States, or in any way abridged, except for participation in rebellion, or other crime, the basis of representation therein shall be reduced in the proportion which the number of such male citizens shall bear to the whole number of male citizens twenty-one years of age in such State.

Section 3. No person shall be a Senator or Representative in Congress, or elector of President and Vice-President, or hold any office, civil or military, under the United States, or under any State, who, having previously taken an oath, as a member of Congress, or as an officer of the United States, or as a member of any State legislature, or as an executive or judicial officer of any State, to support the Constitution of the United States, shall have engaged in insurrection or rebellion against the same, or given aid and comfort to the enemies thereof. But Congress may by a vote of two-thirds of each House, remove such disability.

Section 4. The validity of the public debt of the United States, authorized by law, including debts incurred for payment of pensions and bounties for services in suppressing insurrection and rebellion, shall not be questioned. But neither the United States nor any State shall assume or pay any debt or obligation incurred in aid of insurrection or rebellion against the United States, or any claim for the loss or emancipation of any slave; but all such debts, obligations and claims shall be held illegal and void.

Section 5. The Congress shall have the power to enforce, by appropriate legislation, the provisions of this article.

ARTICLE XV

Section 1. The right of the citizens of the United States to vote shall not be denied or abridged by the United States or by any State on account of race, color, or previous condition of servitude.

Section 2. The Congress shall have power to enforce the provisions of this article by appropriate legislation.

ARTICLE XVI

The Congress shall have power to lay and collect taxes on incomes, from whatever sources derived, without apportionment among the several States, and without regard to any census or enumeration.

ARTICLE XVII

The Senate of the United States shall be composed of two Senators from each State, elected by the people thereof, for six years; and each Senator shall have one vote. The electors in each State shall have the qualifications requisite for electors of the most numerous branch of the State legislature.

When vacancies happen in the representation of any State in the Senate, the executive authority of such State shall issue writs of election to fill such vacancies: *Provided,* That the legislature of any State may empower the executive thereof to make temporary appointment until the people fill the vacancies by election as the legislature may direct.

This amendment shall not be so construed as to affect the election or term of any Senator chosen before it becomes valid as part of the Constitution.

ARTICLE XVIII

Section 1. After one year from the ratification of this article the manufacture, sale, or transportation of intoxicating liquors within, the importation thereof into, or the exportation thereof from the United States and all territory subject to the jurisdiction thereof for beverage purposes is hereby prohibited.

Section 2. The Congress and the several States shall have concurrent power to enforce this article by appropriate legislation.

Section 3. This article shall be inoperative unless it shall have been ratified as an amendment to the Constitution by the legislatures of the several States, as provided in the Constitution, within seven years from the date of the submission hereof to the States by the Congress.

Article XIX

The right of citizens of the United States to vote shall not be denied or abridged by the United States or by any State on account of sex.

Congress shall have power to enforce this article by appropriate legislation.

Article XX

Section 1. The terms of the President and Vice-President shall end at noon on the 20th day of January, and the terms of Senators and Representatives at noon on the 3d day of January, of the years in which such terms would have ended if this article had not been ratified; and the terms of their successors shall then begin.

Section 2. The Congress shall assemble at least once in every year, and such meeting shall begin at noon on the 3d day of January, unless they shall by law appoint a different day.

Section 3. If, at the time fixed for the beginning of the term of the President, the President elect shall have died, the Vice-President elect shall become President. If a President shall not have been chosen before the time fixed for the beginning of his term, or if the President elect shall have failed to qualify, then the Vice-President elect shall act as President until a President shall have qualified, declaring who shall then act as

President, or the manner in which one who is to act shall be selected, and such person shall act accordingly until a President or Vice-President shall have qualified.

Section 4. The Congress may by law provide for the case of the death of any of the persons from whom the House of Representatives may choose a President whenever the right of choice shall have devolved upon them, and for the case of death of any of the persons from whom the Senate may choose a Vice-President whenever the right of choice shall have devolved upon them.

Section 5. Sections 1 and 2 shall take effect on the 15th day of October following the ratification of this article.

Section 6. This article shall be inoperative unless it shall have been ratified as an amendment to the Constitution by the legislatures of three-fourths of the several States within seven years from the date of its submission.

Article XXI

Section 1. The eighteenth article of amendment to the Constitution of the United States is hereby repealed.

Section 2. The transportation or importation into any State, Territory, or Possession of the United States for delivery of use therein of intoxicating liquors, in violation of the laws thereof, is hereby prohibited.

Section 3. This article shall be inoperative unless it shall have been ratified as an amendment to the Constitution by conventions in the several States, as provided in the Constitution, within seven years from the date of the submission hereof to the States by the Congress.

Article XXII

No person shall be elected to the office of the President more than twice, and no person who has held the office of President, or acted as President, for more than two years of a term to which some other person was elected President shall be elected to the office of the President more than once. But this

Article shall not apply to any person holding the office of President when this Article was proposed by the Congress, and shall not prevent any person who may be holding the office of President, or acting as President, during the term within which this Article becomes operative from holding the office of President or acting as President during the remainder of such term.

ARTICLE XXIII

Section 1. The District constituting the seat of Government of the United States shall appoint in such manner as the Congress may direct:

A number of electors of President and Vice President equal to the whole number of Senators and Representatives in Congress to which the District would be entitled if it were a State, but in no event more than the least populous State; they shall be in addition to those appointed by the States, but they shall be considered, for the purposes of the election of President and Vice President, to be electors appointed by a State; and they shall meet in the District and perform such duties as provided by the twelfth article of amendment.

Section 2. The Congress shall have power to enforce this article by appropriate legislation.

NOTE ON SOURCES

THE CLERK of the Constitutional Convention, William Jackson, got $866.60 for his work; and in the opinion of most historians he was overpaid. One of the last things the convention did was instruct him to turn over his Journal and all miscellaneous official papers to George Washington when the session had closed: they didn't know what else to do with them, and they feared that publication at the time might hurt chances of ratification. Washington as well did not know what to do with this mass of documents, and he held on to it for several years until a Congress had been elected, as provided in the Constitution itself; and then he turned the Journal and other papers over to this body. Congress in 1819 caused the Journal to be published, and it aroused no interest at all, being utterly flat and faceless, and in places so laconic as to be almost unintelligible.

Meanwhile very little else about the convention had leaked out, for the delegates by and large appeared to think that their promise of secrecy was to be lifelong, even though the Constitution had been ratified and was in effect. Letters from delegates, usually after the event, and journals and quasi-journals scribbled in the hall and sometimes left like that, sometimes somewhat enlarged upon at night, began to appear; but they appeared slowly, reluctantly, as though shy, and in scattered form. Yates's notes were published in 1821 by his co-delegate, John Lansing, Jr., but Yates had been dead then for twenty years. Lansing's own notes (which had been mislaid) did not see the light of print until 1939. Lansing and Yates, in any event, did not attend the entire convention. Neither did any of the other occasional note-takers—Hamilton, Pierce, McHenry, Luther Martin. Martin's report to the Maryland legislature was the first account to find itself in print, and undoubtedly it had an adverse effect on the ratification; but historians have had little to do with a bit of bombast that is prejudiced to the point of absurdity. Major Pierce's thumbnail sketches of his fellow delegates have been valuable. He had a novelist's eye, and it is a pity that there were not more like him in that hall.

However, by far and away the most valuable source—the work upon which this book is largely based—is the journal James Madison kept so laboriously and so long. *He* was there all the time: he never missed a session. He heard everything, he pondered everything, and he wrote everything down in a shorthand of his own, to be rendered into more conventional and more convenient English that night at his inn while it still was fresh in his mind. He was, in a sense, the real clerk of the convention. Delegates knew what he was doing, and they contributed, reviewing their remarks with him afterward, or giving him a copy of their notes, or when written down, their speeches. Thus, his Journal is more full, at least as reliable, and infinitely more informing than the official one kept by Major Jackson.

Madison was President of the United States from 1809 to 1817. He died in 1836, and the following year his widow, Dolley, sold most of his papers (including the Journal) to the government for $30,000. In 1848 she sold the government some more of her late husband's papers, and these, together with the first batch, were placed in the custody of the Department of State. In 1905 and in 1922—the Journal was in the second transfer—these were deposited in the Library of Congress. The Journal has been published many times, with notes. (*See* MADISON *below; also* ELLIOT) The original is bound in two volumes, one of which is on exhibit in the Library's main building at the present time.

The Birth of the Constitution has not been annotated in detail, because there seemed no need for that. Historians will know at a glance where facts and quotations came from; non-historians are not likely to care. There is no pretense at original research, though there has been an earnest striving for accuracy. The books listed below have been helpful.

Bibliography

ALEXANDER, DeALVA STANWOOD. *A Political History of the State of New York,* 3 volumes. New York: Henry Holt and Company, 1906.

BANCROFT, GEORGE. *History of the Formation of the Constitution of the United States,* 2 volumes. New York: D. Appleton and Company, 1882.

BARRY, JOHN STETSON. *History of Massachusetts,* 3 volumes. Boston: Published by the Author, 1857.

BEARD, CHARLES A. *Economic Interpretation of the Constitution.* New York: The Macmillan Company, 1957.

BECK, JAMES M. *The Constitution of the United States: Yesterday, Today —and Tomorrow?* New York: George H. Doran Company, 1924.

BETHEA, ANDREW J. *The Contribution of Charles Pinckney to the Formation of the American Union.* Richmond: Garret & Massie, Inc., 1937.

BOURNE, EDWARD G. "Authorship of the Federalist." *American Historical Review,* Volume II, Numbers 3 and 4.

BRANT, IRVING. *James Madison: Father of the Constitution, 1787-1800.* Indianapolis: The Bobbs-Merrill Company, 1950.

———. *Storm Over the Constitution.* Indianapolis: The Bobbs-Merrill Company, 1936.

BROWN, ROBERT E. *Charles Beard and the Constitution: A Critical Analysis of "An Economic Interpretation of the Constitution."* Princeton, N.J.: Princeton University Press, 1956.

BROWN, WILLIAM GARROTT. *The Life of Oliver Ellsworth.* New York: The Macmillan Company, 1905.

BURNETT, EDMUND C., editor. *Letters of Members of the Continental Congress,* 8 volumes. Washington: Carnegie Institute of Washington, 1921-36.

BUTZNER, JANE. *Constitutional Chaff: Rejected Suggestions of the Constitutional Convention of 1787, with Explanatory Argument, Compiled from the Notes of James Madison of Virginia, Major William Pierce of Georgia, Dr. James McHenry of Maryland, Rufus King of Massachusetts, and the Honorable Robert Yates of New York.* New York: Columbia University Press, 1941.

CALLAHAN, NORTH. *Henry Knox: General Washington's General.* New York: Rinehart and Company, 1958.

CHANNING, EDWARD. *A History of the United States,* 6 volumes. New York: The Macmillan Company, 1905-25.

COOKE, JACOB E., editor. *The Federalist.* Middletown, Conn.: Wesleyan University Press, 1961.

CURTIS, GEORGE TICKNOR. *History of the Origin, Formation, and Adoption of the Constitution of the United States; with Notices of Its Principal Framers,* 2 volumes. New York: Harper and Brothers, 1854.

CUSHING, HARRY A. *History of the Transition from Provincial to Commonwealth Government in Massachusetts.* New York: Columbia University Press, 1896.

CUSHMAN, ROBERT EUGENE. *Leading Constitutional Decisions.* New York: F. S. Crofts and Company, 1936 (5th edition).

DRAKE, FRANCIS SAMUEL. *Life and Correspondence of Henry Knox.* Boston: S. G. Drake, 1873.

DUNIWAY, CLYDE AUGUSTUS. "French Influence on the Adoption of the Federal Constitution." *American Historical Review,* Volume IX, Number 1.

ELLIOT, JONATHAN. *The Debates in the Several State Conventions on the Adoption of the Federal Constitution as Recommended by the General Convention at Philadelphia in 1787, Together with the Journal of the Federal Convention, Luther Martin's Letter, Yates's Minutes, Congressional Opinions,* 5 volumes. Philadelphia: J. B. Lippincott Company, 1937.

FARRAND, MAX. *Compromises of the Constitution. American Historical Review,* Volume IX.

———. *Framing the Constitution of the United States.* New Haven, Conn.: Yale University Press, 1930.

———. "If James Madison had had a Sense of Humor." Offprint from the *Philadelphia Magazine of History and Biography*, April, 1938.

———. *The Fathers of the Constitution: A Chronicle of the Establishment of the Union*. New Haven, Conn.: Yale University Press, 1921.

FARRAND, MAX, editor. *Rufus King's Notes in Records of the Federal Convention of 1787*.

———. *The Records of the Federal Convention of 1787*, 3 volumes. New Haven, Conn.: Yale University Press, 1911.

FISKE, JOHN. *The Critical Period of American History, 1783-1789*. Boston: Houghton Mifflin and Company, 1898.

FITZPATRICK, JOHN C., *see* WASHINGTON, GEORGE.

FORD, PAUL LEICESTER. "The Authorship of the Federalist." *American Historical Review*, Volume II, Number 4.

FORD, WORTHINGTON CHAUNCEY, editor. *Journals of the Continental Congress 1774-1789*. Washington: Government Printing Office, 1904.

———. *See also* HAMILTON, ALEXANDER.

GANOE, WILLIAM ADDLEMAN. *The History of the United States Army*. New York and London: D. Appleton-Century Company, 1943.

GREENE, EVARTS B. and HARRINGTON, VIRGINIA D. *American Population before the Federal Census of 1790*. New York: Columbia University Press, 1932.

HAMILTON, ALEXANDER. "Alexander Hamilton's Notes on the Convention of 1787," edited by Worthington Chauncey Ford. *American Historical Review*, Volume 10.

HARBISON, WINFRED A., *see* KELLY, ALFRED H.

HARDING, SAMUEL BANNISTER. *The Contest over the Ratification of the Federal Constitution in the State of Massachusetts*. New York: Longmans, Green, and Company, 1896.

HARRINGTON, VIRGINIA D., *see* GREENE, EVARTS B.

HOFSTADTER, RICHARD. "Beard and the Constitution: The History of an Idea." *American Quarterly*, Fall 1950.

———. *The American Political Tradition*. New York: Alfred A. Knopf, 1954.

HOLLAND, JOSIAH GILBERT. *History of Western Massachusetts*, 2 volumes. Springfield, Mass.: Samuel Bowles and Company, 1855.

HUNT, GAILLARD, *see* MADISON, JAMES.

JACKSON, WILLIAM, editor. *Journal, Acts and Proceedings of the Convention, Assembled at Philadelphia, Monday, May 14, and Dissolved Monday, September 17, 1787*.

JAMESON, JOHN ALEXANDER. *The Constitutional Convention: It's History, Powers, and Modes of Proceeding*. New York: Charles Scribner and Company, 1867.

JAMESON, J. F. "Did the Fathers Vote?" *The New England Magazine*, January 1890.

JENSEN, MERRILL. *The Articles of Confederation: An Interpretation of the Social-Constitutional History of the American Revolution, 1774-1781.* Madison, Wis.: University of Wisconsin Press, 1940.

KELLY, ALFRED H. and HARBISON, WINFRED A. *The American Constitution: Its Origins and Development.* New York: W. W. Norton & Co., 1955.

KING, CHARLES RUFUS. *The Life and Correspondence of Rufus King, Comprising His Letters, Private and Official, His Public Documents, and His Speeches,* 4 volumes. New York: G. P. Putnam's Sons, 1897.

LANSING, JOHN, JR. *The Delegate from New York, or Proceedings of the Federal Convention of 1787,* edited by JOSEPH REESE STRAYER. Princeton: Princeton University Press, 1939.

LIBBY, ORIN GRANT. *The Geographical Distribution of the Vote of the Thirteen States on the Federal Constitution, 1787-8.* Madison, Wis.: University of Wisconsin Press, 1894.

LYON, HASTINGS. *The Constitution and the Men Who Made It: The Story of the Constitutional Convention, 1787.* Boston: Houghton Mifflin Company, 1936.

MCDONALD, FORREST. *We the People: The Economic Origins of the Constitution.* Chicago: The University of Chicago Press, 1958.

MCLAUGHLIN, ANDREW CUNNINGHAM. *The Confederation and the Constitution, 1783-1789.* New York: Harper and Brothers, 1905.

MADISON, JAMES. *Journal of the Federal Convention,* 2 volumes, edited by E. H. SCOTT. Chicago: Albert, Scott and Company, 1894.

————. *The Debates in the Federal Convention of 1787 Which Framed the Constitution of the United States of America,* edited by Gaillard Hunt and James Brown Scott. New York: Oxford University Press, 1920.

————. *The Writings of James Madison,* 9 volumes, edited by Gaillard Hunt. New York: G. P. Putnam's Sons, 1900.

MAIN, JACKSON TURNER. *The Antifederalists: Critics of the Constitution, 1781-1788.* Chapel Hill: University of North Carolina Press, 1961.

MARTYN, CHARLES. *The Life of Artemas Ward, the First Commander-in-Chief of the American Revolution.* New York: Artemas Ward, 1921.

MINER, C. E. *The Ratification of the Federal Constitution by the State of New York.* New York: Columbia University Press, 1921.

MINOT, GEORGE RICHARDS. *The History of Insurrections in Massachusetts in the Year Seventeen Hundred and Eighty Six and the Rebellion Consequent Thereon.* Boston: James W. Burditt & Co., 1810.

MORSE, JOHN T., JR. *Benjamin Franklin.* Boston: Houghton Mifflin Co., 1891.

NEVINS, ALLAN. *The American States During and After the Revolution, 1775-1789.* New York: The Macmillan Company, 1927.

OLIVER, FREDERICK SCOTT. *Alexander Hamilton: An Essay on American Union.* New York: G. P. Putnam's Sons, 1907.

PATERSON, WILLIAM. "Papers of William Paterson on the Federal Convention, 1787." *American Historical Review IX.*

PIERCE, WILLIAM. "Notes of Major William Pierce on the Federal Convention of 1787." *American Historical Review III.*

PRESCOTT, ARTHUR TAYLOR. *Drafting the Federal Constitution: A Rearrangement of Madison's Notes Giving Consecutive Developments of Provisions in the Constitution of the United States, Supplemented by Documents Pertaining to the Philadelphia Convention and to Ratification Processes, and Including Insertions by the Compiler.* Baton Rouge: Louisiana State University Press, 1941.

PRITCHETT, HERMAN. *The American Constitution.* New York: The McGraw-Hill Book Company, Inc., 1959.

RODELL, FRED. *Fifty-Five Men.* New York: The Telegraph Press, 1936.

ROOSEVELT, THEODORE. *Gouverneur Morris.* Boston: Houghton, Mifflin and Company, 1891.

RUTLAND, ROBERT ALLEN. *The Birth of the Bill of Rights, 1776-1791.* Chapel Hill: University of North Carolina Press, 1955.

SCHACHNER, NATHAN. *Alexander Hamilton.* New York: D. Appleton-Century Company, 1946.

SCOTT, E. H., *see* MADISON, JAMES.

SCOTT, JAMES BROWN, *see* MADISON, JAMES.

STRAYER, JOSEPH REESE, *see* LANSING, JOHN, JR.

SWIGGETT, HOWARD. *The Extraordinary Mr. Morris.* Garden City, N.Y.: Doubleday and Co., 1952.

TANSILL, CHARLES CALLAN, editor. *Documents Illustrative of the Formation of the Union of the American States.* Washington: Government Printing Office, 1927.

TWISS, BENJAMIN R. *Lawyers and the Constitution: How Laissez Faire Came to the Supreme Court.* Foreword by Edward S. Corwin. Princeton: Princeton University Press, 1942.

TYLER, MOSES COIT. *Patrick Henry.* Boston: Houghton Mifflin Co., 1898.

VAN DOREN, CARL. *Benjamin Franklin.* New York: The Viking Press, 1938.
———. *The Great Rehearsal: The Story of the Making and Ratifying of the Constitution of the United States.* New York: The Viking Press, 1948.

WARREN, CHARLES. *The Making of the Constitution.* Boston: Little, Brown and Company, 1928.

WARREN, JOSEPH PARKER. "The Confederation and the Shays' Rebellion." *American Historical Review,* Volume XI, Number 1.

WASHINGTON, GEORGE. *The Writings of George Washington, from the Original Manuscript Sources, 1745-1799,* 39 volumes, edited by JOHN C. FITZPATRICK. Washington: Government Printing Office, 1931-44.

WESTCOTT, THOMPSON. *Life of John Fitch, the Inventor of the Steam-Boat.* Philadelphia: J. B. Lippincott & Co., 1857.

WILSON, FRED TAYLOR. *Our Constitution and Its Makers.* New York: Leming H. Revell Company, 1937.

YATES, ROBERT. *Secret Proceedings and Debates of the Convention Assembled at Philadelphia, in the Year 1787.* Cincinnati: Alston Mygatt, 1838.

———, *see also* ELLIOTT, JONATHAN.

Index